ACING DIGITAL MARKETING

A ROADMAP TO DIGITAL MARKETING

DR. GYANANDRE TRIPATHI
DR. ABHISHIKHA PATEL

INDIA • SINGAPORE • MALAYSIA

ISBN 979-8-89067-723-5

CONTENTS

INTRODUCTION TO DIGITAL MARKETING

"The internet is becoming the town square for the global village tomorrow"

— **Bill Gates**

OVERVIEW OF DIGITAL MARKETING

The term digital marketing refers to the use of digital channels to market products and services in order to reach consumers. Digital marketing became popular with the advent of the internet in the 1990s. Marketing refers to activities that a company uses to promote its products and services and improve its market share. Corporations traditionally focused on marketing through print, television, and radio. digital marketing involves the use of websites, social media, search engines, and apps—anything that incorporates marketing with customer feedback or a two-way interaction between the company and its customers.

MEANING OF DIGITAL MARKETING

Digital marketing involves marketing to consumers through any number of digital channels, including websites, mobile devices, and social media platforms. Digital marketing is a broad field, including attracting customers via email, content marketing, search platforms, social media, and more.

DEFINITION OF DIGITAL MARKETING

Marketing component that promotes products and services via the Internet and online-based digital technologies such as desktop computers, mobile phones, and other digital media and platforms.

TRADITIONAL MARKETING

Traditional marketing is any form of marketing that reaches an audience through offline media. Newspaper ads and other print advertisements are basic examples of traditional marketing, but there are also billboards, mail advertisements, and TV and radio advertisements.

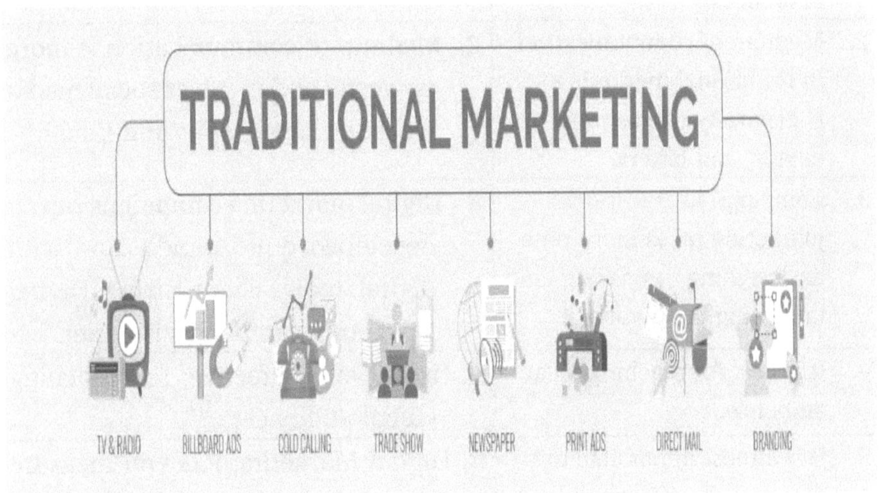

DIFFERENCES FROM TRADITIONAL MARKETING

Traditional marketing allows businesses to market their products or services through print media, radio and TV commercials, billboards, business cards, and a variety of other comparable methods where the Internet or web-based social networking sites were not used for promotion.

Traditional marketing includes tangible items such as business cards, print ads in newspapers or magazines. It can also include posters, commercials on TV and radio, billboards and brochures. Traditional marketing is anything except digital means to brand your product or logo.

Traditional Marketing	Digital Marketing
1. Communication is unidirectional in traditional marketing, which means, an organization communicates about its services with its audiences.	1. Communication is bidirectional in Digital Marketing as businesses can communicate with customers and customers can ask queries or make suggestions to businesses as well.
2. Medium of communication in traditional marketing is generally phone calls, emails, and letters.	2. Medium of communication is more powerful and involves social media websites, chats, apps and Email.
3. Campaign in Traditional marketing takes more time as designing, preparing, and launching are involved.	3. Digital marketing campaigns can be developed quite rapidly and with digital tools, channelizing Digital Marketing campaigns is easier.
4. It is best for reaching local audience.	4. It is very effective for reaching global audiences.
5. It is almost impossible to measure the effectiveness of a traditional marketing campaign.	5. Digital Marketing lets you measure the effectiveness of a digital marketing campaign through analytics.

Digital Marketing's overall concept and functionalities are more competent, effective, result-oriented, and measurable, distinguishing it from traditional marketing. Digital marketing includes things like websites, social media mentions, YouTube videos, and banner ads. Specifically, digital marketing is similar to traditional advertising, but using digital devices. One benefit to using digital marketing is that the results are much easier to measure; and another is that a digital campaign can reach an infinite audience. Benefits of Digital Marketing over Traditional Marketing include reduced cost, real time result, brand Development, non-intrusive, higher exposure, higher engagement, Quicker publicity, Non interruptive, Good for All Stages of Fields, Easy analytics and Strategy Refinement. One of the disadvantages to using digital media marketing strategies is that it can take some time to realize measurable success.

RETURN OF INVESTMENTS ON DIGITAL MARKETING VS TRADITIONAL MARKETING

Traditional marketing usually includes some kind of physical deliverable that you can see, touch or hear, such as TV and radio commercials, print ads, direct mail, and more. Traditional marketing has numerous benefits, including its ability to reach a wide audience and its tangibility. And, because traditional marketing can be seen, heard or touched, it can be very persuasive in convincing customers to make a purchase. Some of its drawbacks include high costs, low flexibility and turnaround time. Because traditional marketing can be costly, it is often only used to reach a specific audience — one that is already interested in what you have to offer.

Digital marketing is the process of using online channels to promote and sell products or services. This can include search engine optimization (SEO), pay-per-click (PPC) advertising, social media marketing, email marketing, and more. Digital marketing has become increasingly popular over recent years because it offers multiple benefits over traditional methods. For one, you can reach a wider audience with digital marketing than you can with traditional marketing. Additionally, there is little to no cost for creating material to advertise products online and few limits on where these advertisements can be placed.

Measuring your investment return can help you determine which marketing activities are worth your time and resources. Plus, understanding your ROI can help you make more informed decisions about allocating your marketing budget. There are several ways to calculate ROI, but the most basic ROI formula looks something like this:

ROI = (Marketing revenue – spend) / Marketing spend x 100

For example, if you generate $3,000 in revenue from a campaign that costs $2,000 to run, your marketing will have produced a 50%

return on investment. There are many other factors to consider, such as customer satisfaction, brand awareness, and engagement.

There is no easy answer when deciding between digital marketing and traditional marketing. Both have their pros and cons, and ultimately the best strategy is usually a mix of both. However, digital marketing is often the way to go if you are looking for the best ROI. With its lower costs and higher reach, digital marketing can help you get more profits.

E-COMMERCE

E-commerce (electronic commerce) is the activity of electronically buying or selling of products on online services or over the Internet. E-commerce allows customers to choose a product or service they want, from any supplier, anywhere in the world.

E-commerce is the process of selling goods and services over the internet. Customers come to the website or online marketplace and purchase products using electronic payments. Upon receiving the money, the merchant ships the goods or provides the service. E-commerce customers and businesses can save time and money. It enables sellers to sell to a global audience and also customers to make a global choice.

Geographical boundaries and challenges are eradicated/drastically reduced. Through direct interaction with final customers, this e-commerce process cuts the product distribution chain to a significant extent. The Indian E-Commerce market is expected to reach $170 billion by 2025. India's online shopper base is to reach nearly 500-600 million by 2030 and become the 2nd largest globally. One of the main limitations of E-Commerce is security.

Amazon.in is the most visited E-commerce and Retail website in India in December 2022, attracting nearly 335.5M monthly visits.

There are three main types of e-commerce: business-to-business (websites such as Shopify), business-to-consumer (websites such as Amazon), and consumer-to-consumer (websites such as eBay).

TOOLS USED FOR SUCCESSFUL MARKETING

The vast majority of businesses use several different marketing tools, such as advertising, direct mail, and market research to boost their sales. Companies have a range of marketing tools at their disposal. Some of them are specifically for boosting sales, while others focus on gathering consumer data. Digital marketing can be broadly broken into 8 main categories including: Search Engine Optimization, Pay-per-Click, Social Media Marketing, Content Marketing, Email Marketing, Mobile Marketing, Marketing Analytics and Affiliate Marketing. Digital marketing, also called online marketing, is the promotion of brands to connect with potential customers using the internet and other forms of digital communication. This includes not only email, social media, and web-based advertising, but also text and multimedia messages as a marketing channel.

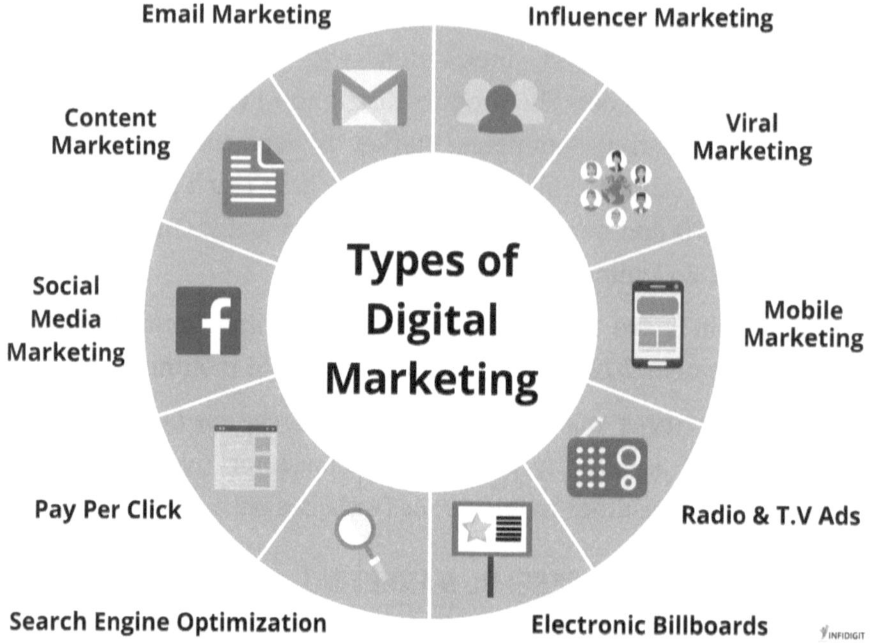

The four Ps are product, price, place, and promotion. They are an example of a "marketing mix," or the combined tools and methodologies used by marketers to achieve their marketing objectives. The 4 Cs, or the four pillars of the marketing mix, are a modern twist on the traditional 4 P's.

These principles focus on customer value, convenience, communication, and cost-efficiency. The 4 C's of Marketing Are Customer, Cost, Convenience, and Communication.

These 4 C's determine whether a company is likely to succeed or fail in the long run. Almost every digital marketing activity falls into one of six types: content marketing, SEO, search engine marketing, social media marketing, affiliates and influencers, and email and message marketing.

- Product- Product is the first P in the marketing mix and is defined as physical goods or services sold to make a profit for the business.

- Place -Place in the marketing mix encompasses the entire process of taking a product from the manufacturer and making it accessible to the consumer, which can include all intermediaries and distributors. This can include both in-person and online places, such as storefronts and websites.

- Price- Price in marketing mix refers to the value we pay in exchange for the product and services offered by a company. Price is considered a vital element of the marketing mix because it dictates a company's survival and profit. Pricing of a product plays an important role in determining the success of a company.

- Promotion- Promotion is a marketing tool, used as a strategy to communicate between the sellers and buyers. Through this, the seller tries to influence and convince the buyers to buy their products or services.

- Customer- Customer mix is the sales driven by a particular type of customer segment expressed as a percentage of business's total sale.

- Cost - Marketing costs are the all expenses that the company makes to market and sell its products and develop and promote its brand. These marketing costs or expenses include expenses incurred to change the title of goods, promotion of goods, inventory costs, distribution of goods etc.

- Convenience - convenience means that you make it easy, simple, and fast for your customers to avail of your product(s) or service(s).

- Communication- The marketing communication mix is a set of advertising, personal selling, publicity, public relations, digital PR, etc. that companies use to fulfil their marketing goals. It is directly responsible for delivering your promotional message using various communication channels.

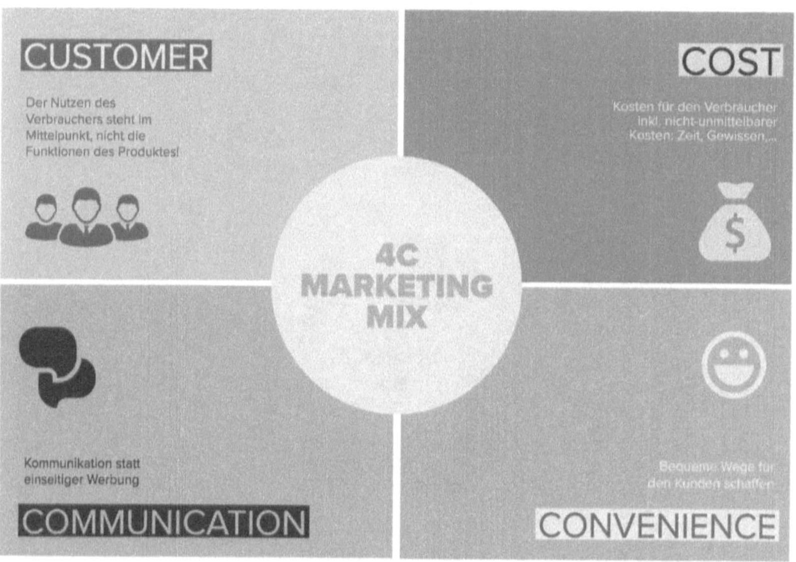

BRIEF ABOUT TOOLS USED IN DIGITAL MARKETING-

- content marketing- One of the key objectives of modern digital marketing is to raise brand awareness. Content marketing is a marketing strategy used to attract, engage, and retain an audience by creating and sharing relevant articles, videos, podcasts, and other media. This approach establishes expertise, promotes brand awareness, and keeps your business top of mind when it's time to buy what you sell.

Expert Articles and Guides	Guest Blogging	Product Updates	Share Exciting Data
Job Listings	Case studies and whitepapers	Industry and company news	Interviews and Surveys
Community-driven content	Customer Showcases	Updated Product pages	Influencers for Content

- SEO- SEO stands for "search engine optimization." In simple terms, SEO means the process of improving your website to increase its visibility in Google, Microsoft Bing, and other search engines whenever people search for: Products you sell.

- search engine marketing- Search engine marketing is a form of Internet marketing that involves the promotion of websites by increasing their visibility in search engine results pages primarily through paid advertising.

- social media marketing- Social media marketing is the use of social media platforms and websites to promote a product or service. Social media marketing (SMM) (also known as digital marketing and e-marketing) is the use of social media—the platforms on which users build social networks and share information—to build a company's brand, increase sales, and drive website traffic.

- affiliates and influencers- affiliate marketing involves referring a product or service by sharing it on a blog, social media platforms, or website. The affiliate earns a commission each time someone makes a purchase through the unique link or code associated with their recommendation.

- Influencer marketing involves brands collaborating with online influencers to market products or services.

- email and message marketing- Email marketing is a form of marketing that can make the customers on your email list aware of new products, discounts, and other services.

Text message marketing involves using Short Message Service (SMS) messages to deliver advertising and other content directly to mobile devices.

SWOT ANALYSIS OF BUSINESS FOR DIGITAL MARKETING

A SWOT analysis is a framework that marketing teams used to identify their internal strengths and weaknesses, and the external factors that could be affecting the way that their organization is running. The strength of digital marketing is the massage easy to target and reach more audience a cheaper price in the consumers. Then another one is weakness of digital marketing it's refer to a challenges to reach the population which is still not using the internet in this aspect weakness of digital marketing in India.

5 steps for a professional SWOT analysis

Step 1: Analyse trends, industry, customers & competitors. No matter if the SWOT is done for a start-up, corporate strategy or just a project. ...

Step 2: Identify strengths & weaknesses. ...

Step 3: Derive opportunities and risks. ...

Step 4: Develop measures. ...

Step 5: Adapt and update.

Common business strengths

- Unique product or knowledge.

- Excellent efficiency and productivity.

- Customer service that creates raving fan customers.

- Speed to market.

- High adaptability.

- Diversification of products or services.

- Strong, decisive leadership.

Examples of weaknesses for a SWOT analysis might include lack of motivation, lack of a clear vision, or poor time management skills.

Opportunity examples for businesses include market growth, new technologies, or new investments.

They can include:

- Weather- These affect seasonal businesses that depend on good conditions.

- The economy-If you sell something consumers need in any economy, you will fare better than others.

- Material shortage. ...

- Your computer system is hacked. ...

- Employment in your industry is strong. ...

- Market demand dries up.

MEANING OF BLOGS, WEBSITES, PORTAL AND THEIR DIFFERENCES

Dictionary meaning of Blog is a website where a person writes regularly about topics that interest them, usually with photographs and links to other websites they find interesting.

A blog (a shortened version of "weblog") is an online journal or informational website displaying information in reverse chronological order, with the latest posts appearing first, at the top.

It is a platform where a writer or a group of writers share their views on an individual subject.

The purpose of blog is for creating a relationship between a company and its audience. It can also provide knowledge on relevant topics, increase engagement and traffic to your website, and create a community. If done correctly, it can help create a thriving foundation for corresponding social media platforms.

The most common types of blogs are:

- Personal blogs.

- Business/corporate blogs.

- Personal brand/professional blogs.

- Fashion blogs.

- Blog newsletter.

- Lifestyle blogs.

- Travel blogs.

- Food blogs.

Common uses include teaching and educational and corporate use. Blog can be a personal diary, a project collaboration tool, a guide, or any means of communicating and publishing information on the web.

10 main characteristics and features of a blog

- A Blog Must Always Be Dynamic. ...

- Posts Are Displayed in Reverse Order. ...

- Most Blogs Have the Same Structure. ...

- The Blog's Leading Star Is Its Content. ...

- Headlines Should Be Attention Grabbers. ...

- One Rule Applies to All Blogs: Relevancy. ...

- Blogs and Links Go Hand in Hand.

A blog structure is an essential foundation for writing a blog article, containing the title, intro, body, and conclusion.

MEANING OF WEBSITES

Dictionary meaning of website is that a place connected to the Internet, where a company, organization, etc. puts information that can be found on the World Wide Web.

A website is a collection of publicly accessible, interlinked Web pages that share a single domain name. Websites can be created and maintained by an individual, group, business or organization to serve a variety of purposes. Websites are hosted on servers, and require a web browser such as Chrome, Firefox, or Internet Explorer to be visited (either on a computer or mobile device). A website can be accessed directly by entering its URL address or by searching it on a search engine such as Google or Bing.

Originally, websites were categorized by their top-level domains. Some examples include:

- Government agency websites = .gov

- Educational institutions' websites = .edu

- Nonprofit organizations' websites = .org

- Commercial websites = .com

- Information sites = .info

In modern days' internet, the ".com" extension is by far the most popular domain, together with many other country-specific extensions (.it, .de, .co.uk, .fr, etc.).

Top 10 Benefits of Having a Website

- Online Presence 24/7.

- Information Exchange.

- Credibility.

- It Cuts Costs.

- Market Expansion.

- Consumer Insights.

- Advertising.

- Competitors Online.

6 Essential Features Every Website Should Have

- A Simple, Easy to Remember URL: ...

- A Clear Description of Your Business: ...

- Call to Actions: ...

- Contact Information: ...

- Mobile Friendly or Responsive Design: ...

- Staff Photos and Biographies

The most important part to any website is content. Without content, your website is nothing more than an advertisement, which is not an effective online marketing strategy. Generally, the purpose of most websites are: Awareness, sales, and information. A website is a collection of related material that contains text, images, and may also include video, audio or other media.

The Difference between Webpage and Website is that "The webpage is a single document on the web using a unique URL, while a website is a collection of multiple webpages in which information on a related topic or another subject is linked together under the same domain address."

Hyper Text Markup Language (HTML) is the most popular mark-up language in the world, and it is a must-learn for front-end web developers.

MEANING OF PORTAL

Dictionary meaning of portal is a website that is used as a point of entry to the Internet, where information has been collected that will be useful to a person interested in particular kinds of things.

Portal is a term, generally synonymous with gateway, door, entrance.

A portal is a web-based platform that collects information from different sources into a single user interface and presents users with the most relevant information for their context.

Over time, simple web portals have evolved into portal platforms that support digital customer experience initiatives. A portal represents a web site that provides a single point of access to applications and information.

The web portal is important to ease the business options and improve its efficiency as much as possible.

Businesses prefer to have the one-stop point for the organization of data and other business chores.

Portals provide a way for enterprises and organizations to provide a consistent "look and feel" with access control and procedures for multiple applications and databases, which otherwise would have been different web entities at various URLs.

Some of the most favoured web portals are:

- Educational portal.

- Financial portal.

- Government portal.

- Employee portal.

- Patient portal.

- Retail banking portal.

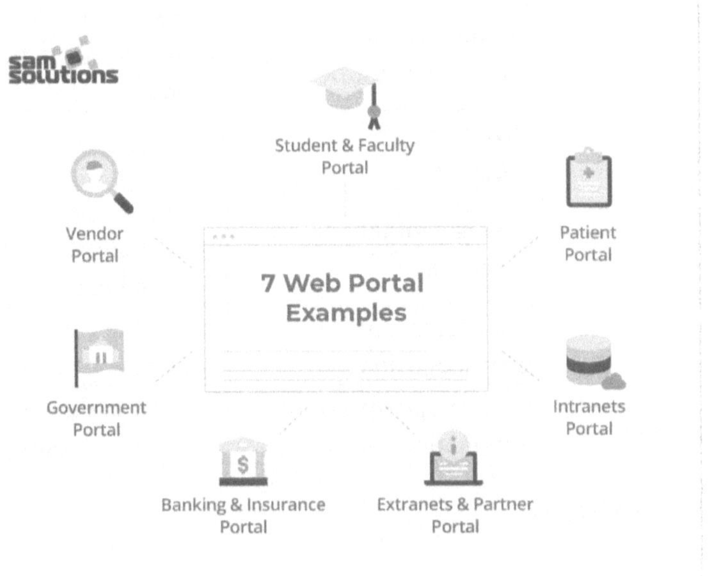

DIFFERENCE between BLOGS, WEBSITES, PORTAL

A website is a location present on the internet with various web pages that one can access via its URL. A web portal is a point of access in which the content is only available for a set of specific users.

DIFFERENCE Between WEBSITE and PORTAL

Website and Portal are distinct terms, but there exists a correlation between the two. Website and portal both have a web-based interface; a website is the collection of web pages whereas a portal act as a gateway to world wide web and provides many services.

An organization owns a website. On the other hand, a portal is user-centric which means a user can probably provide information and data.

COMPARISON CHART

Basis For Comparison	Website	Portal
Basic	It is a location on the internet usually accessed through an URL.	It provides a single point of access where the traffic is limited to the right set of users.
Features	Owned by an organization.	User-centric.
Interaction	User cannot interact with a website.	There is a two-way communication between user and portal.
Property	Not necessarily a knowledge domain.	Act as the gateway to the specific knowledge domain.
Management	Seldom updating of the information sources.	Regular updating of information sources.

Definition of Website

A **website** is the group of web pages which are placed in a location on the internet and accessed through a web address. Content on a website is globally visible, publically used, remains same for the different individuals. Users need not to login for accessing the website. The user can perform any specific task, and the website supports it.

A website could be industry-specific, product specific or services specific etc.; these websites are intended to educate their site visitors about their industry, products or services information. There is no use of a personalized database, and the website does not usually reference it.

Definition of Portal

A web **portal** is a typical knowledge management system that delivers the facility for organisation or companies to build, share, interchange and reuse knowledge. It is the private location on the internet retrieved through a unique URL (web address), and probably login id and password.

Web portal content is login protected and user specific and its interface could be public and private.

It allows access to multiple user roles. Contents in a web portal are dynamic and changed frequently. The visibility of one content changes from person to person which means a content could be unique to a user based on group member settings. Contents are collected from the different and diverse sources.

Portals can be divided into two classes: **Horizontal portals** (Horizontal Enterprise Portals) and **vertical portals** (Vertical Enterprise Portals).

- Horizontal portals are analogous to a public website which tries to deliver every type of service that its users may need.

- Vertical portals work in a user-centric manner and deliver information that is organization-specific.

Key Differences Between Website and Portal

- A website is a set of interlinked web pages hosted from the same domain, which can be accessed through a web address. As against a portal is a custom-made website which involves information from a broad class of sources in a persistent manner.

- A portal is usually user-centric whereas a website is owned by an organization or company etc.

- There is no intercommunication between the website and the user. On the contrary, a user can interact with the portal.

- A website is not a primary knowledge domain whereas portal is the passage to knowledge management system.

- The information is regularly updated in case of a portal. In contrast, the information sources in a website are rarely updated.

Difference Between Website and Blog

The Website and Blogs are somewhat similar. There are very few differences between them, but these are differentiable. The major difference between website and blog is that a blog is more interactive, while a website is static or inactive.

If we talk about blogs, the content of the blogs is frequently changed, and these are capable of providing the fresh and updated content each time a viewer visits the blog after a period of time. Conversely, this is not the case with the websites. The contents in the other websites (that are not informational websites) rarely changes.

COMPARISON CHART

Basis For Comparison	Website	Blog
Fundamental unit	Content	Post
Order	No order	Chronological
Commenting	Not always possible	Enabled
Subscription	No subscription is available to the RSS feed.	One can subscribe to the blog's RSS feed.
Updating frequency	Rare	Often
Home page	Could be present	Mandatorily present

Definition of Website

A **website** has a web page that is comprised of embedded text with resources like links, hypertext, forms, sound, images, etc. The objective of a website is to drive together with the resources and deliver the information to the viewer in an understandable, impressive and creative way. However, the information provided is regarding a specific purpose.

For example, if someone has a specific purpose or objective to write a book on some topic, then he/she could successfully accomplish it. Similarly, for constructing a website, you must define a specific objective or purpose.

Definition of Blog

In a technical sense, a **blog** is also a type of website. It is an open-source content management system or a blogging tool that runs on a hosting system. It is a short form of a weblog, which can be defined as the online journal shared over the internet. With the help of a blog, one can post diary entries related to his/her personal experiences or interests.

A blog is created and edited by an individual known as the blogger. To maintain a blog, one should focus on publishing the post to the internet using blog technology and updating the blogging program and its characteristics.

Key Differences Between Website and Blog

1. The website is more general term as compared to a blog, which is more specifically designed. In other words, all blogs are considered to be a website, but not all websites are considered to be blog.

2. The basic unit in a website is content, whereas, in a blog, it is a post.

3. In a blog (or informational websites), the contents are placed according to some chronological order. As against, on a website, there is no specific arrangement of the contents followed.

4. The commenting section is mostly provided in the blogs, while this is not necessary with the websites as the blogs are more interactive than a website.

5. The homepage could probably be present within a blog, but on the website, the homepage should be included.

VISIBILITY

In business, visibility refers to the extent to which a company can estimate its future performance. While it is a very broad term that applies to both short-term and long-term performance, having visibility into the organization greatly helps management to run a business better.

Visibility can be defined as a metric showing how often your website is found on the Internet. here are a handful of reasons why online visibility is important: It lets users find your site on their own. Unique visitors, or new daily visitors, are customers supporting your business. Online visibility helps with brand reputation, or how a business is perceived in the marketplace.

To Increase Search Engine Visibility in 12 Simple Ways

1. Optimize Existing Content. ...

2. Update Evergreen Content. ...

3. Focus on Long-tail Keywords. ...

4. Increase the Amount of High-Quality Content. ...

5. Add More Engaging Multimedia. ...

6. Compose Better Meta Tags. ...

7. Consider Adding More Internal Links. ...

8. Build a Backlinking Strategy.

In digital marketing, online visibility or online presence refers to how much attention, or awareness, your business has online. This means where your brand shows up on the internet, across different digital channels. Today, just because you have a website doesn't mean it's visible to the right audience. One of the best ways to increase visibility on Google is to track and monitor keyword ranking. Many SEOs use Google Search Console for this purpose.

10 steps for increasing visibility in digital marketing.

1. Establish Your Brand's Website.

2. Create a Blog.

3. Make SEO a Priority.

4. Don't Forget About Off-Site SEO.

5. Utilize Social Media.

6. Capitalize On Email Marketing.

7. Invest in Paid Ads.

8. Encourage Online Customer Reviews.

VISITOR ENGAGEMENT

Engagement Marketing is all about building relationships together with your customers. The visitor engagement is about boosting and attracting customers to engage in the evolution of their brand or brand experience. It's known when brand and customer connect.

The lack of visitor engagement will result in a lack of conversions as you were hoping for when first posting and promoting new content. Unfortunately, there are several different reasons visitors might not be engaging together with your site.

Methods of Visitor Engagement:

There are some key actions to extend the amount of returning visitors. To try to do this, it's necessary to supply content which will engage, create loyalty, and always be in touch together with your audience. The content is defined by its purpose to be created. That purpose is getting casual readers to subscribe to your email list more often than not, but it could even be getting them to shop for or download a product.

- **Simple Navigation**

    The marketplace is crowded and noisy, to mention the smallest amount. The simplest websites embrace a minimalist approach, going with simple and stylish. When it involves UX and website navigation, less could also be better.

    Leverage a neat and easy layout with limited widgets, boxes, callouts and pop-ups. Reduce the quantity of CTAs on your pages to direct users toward what you would like them to try to. Produce easy-to-understand navigation bars with collapsed menus by theme or sections. Be conscientious of clutter use white space where you'll.

- **Switch to HTTPS**

  First thing firsts, the most concern for users will always be the safety of your website. it's easy to know why. HTTP stands for Hypertext Transfer Protocol. The HTTP in HTTPS is that the same, the extra S stands for Secure. Therefore, switching to HTTPS lets users comprehend which your website is secure. They're going to stay your website and explore freely, not having to stress about anything.

  If your website is using HTTP, Google will show that your website isn't secure and warn users to not key in important and sensitive data like password and credit cards on your website.

- **Add Videos**

  If you don't want to feature much content to your website, then create videos that cover subjects written and embed them into your site. The graphic designer can show the merchandise features in videos or animation form alongside highlighting your offering.

  A major aspect of web typography also plays an important role. It's all about how you employ different fonts, letters, words & paragraphs on the webpages for a display to make an aesthetic feeling among visitors.

- **Optimize for Speed & Responsiveness**

  If your website is slow, potential consumers might drive their business away. Beyond that, site speed is a crucial Google ranking factor when it involves attracting organic traffic to your site.

  Therefore, one among the primary moves you create in upping your website engagement should be optimizing your site speed and responsiveness. To stop this from happening, you ought to work with a developer or your chosen service provider to hurry up your site and optimize it for mobile.

- **Collect Email Addresses**

  Blog traffic won't assist you if those visitors leave and never return. That's why it's important to capture their email addresses so you'll stay in-tuned. Growing your email list is important to put together a community for your business. And email marketing is one among the most important money-makers.

  Collecting email addresses will allow you to bring **targeted traffic in digital marketing.** Then later on speak to them directly any time you've got something to mention. If you would like to market a product or announce a purchase, an email list is that the best thanks to roll in the hay.

- **Use Notifications**

  In the digital world, businesses should retain themselves renewed with trending methods. Using push or mobile notifications is one among the simplest techniques which may be wont to engage your users on both web and mobile.

  Push notifications provide a more powerful amount of conversion rates than many other techniques. It will assist to heighten through website engagement. The great thing is that the user doesn't need to get on your website or mobile app to receive these notifications that mean you'll engage them anytime.

- **Make Sign-up Easy**

  Encourage and facilitate visitor sign-ups for your website offerings and your company will enjoy a transparent conversion path to new customers. The simplest conversion path features several calls-to-action, i.e. "Sign-up Today" or other verbs on links/buttons.

An artfully crafted landing page will convince visitors to require meaningful action within the sort of requesting more information or making a sale. All of those points encompass the crucial pieces to your website puzzle!

- **Lengthen Your Text**

Studies show that pages with 1,000 to 2,500 words tend to experience the very best user engagement. It is sensible as the higher amount of words there is, the longer site visitors will spend reading.

Don't expand your text with fluff, but do your best to supply quality, informative, and actionable content that gives value to your visitors' lives. That's the sort of content today's site visitors is more apt to interact with.

- **Add Content Upgrades**

A content upgrade is an exceptional way to captivate potential customers especially the ones who might not be quite ready to buy. You can snag their email address and market to them until they are ready to make a purchase.

Discounts are one popular content upgrade for websites, but there are many others. The key is to provide something your potential customers will find value in something they are willing to hand their email addresses over for.

CONVERSION PROCESS

Conversion marketing is a digital marketing strategy that focuses on increasing the percentage of site visitors who perform a specific action, called a conversion. Often, conversion refers to a customer making a purchase, though the desired action can instead be signing up for a webinar or filling out a form. a conversion is "the point at which a recipient of a marketing message performs a desired action." In other words, a conversion is simply getting someone to respond to your call-to-action. In paid advertising, conversion is the ultimate goal, and naturally, it is the final step in the Pay-Per-Click (PPC) process.

Google Ads defines a conversion as: "An action that is counted when somebody interacts with an ad (e.g. when they click a text ad or view a video ad), and then they take an action you have defined as valuable to your business, such as making an online purchase or a phone call to your business from their mobile phone"

From that, we can deduce that a conversion is not solely limited to online purchases. Indeed, conversions can take many forms.

- For a masseuse, a phone call from a customer to book an appointment is a successful conversion.

- For an eBook website, every download of an eBook is a successful conversion.

- For an ecommerce website, any online purchase is a successful conversion.

- Essentially, conversions are the return on investment (ROI) for your spending. It's absolutely imperative that you track this if you are to have any hope of gauging true performance of your campaign.

- Moreover, only by tracking ROI can you look for ways to improve it. Multiple factors affect your return, and Google Ads provide enough campaign data for you to discover:

- your total conversions

- The number of users that converted after visiting your website

- Whether the conversion is costing you more than your profit

- Your total Ads cost, and whether it's viable to keep running ads

- The total cost per conversion

- Your most profitable traffic sources

- The number of people that leave your site immediately after arriving. This lets you know if your ads are relevant or not.

7 Metrics to Track Conversions in the PPC Process

With everything from the last section in mind, let's look at the metrics that you can study to find out how to make your conversion strategy more efficient and cost-effective.

1. Conversions

It is a simple one to start. This is the total number of conversions you've received to date on a specific goal, which you have identified as a conversion in your ad campaign.

2. Conversion Rate

This shows you how many users visited your website or landing page and then converted, compared to the total number of visits to that page.

Conversion Rate = Total Conversions / Total number of visitors

The conversion rate lets you gauge performance on your pages. If it's poor, you should look to identify the problems and correct them. It's a smart move to pause your ads until you do this, as it will save your budget.

3. Conversion Value

Some conversions are more valuable than others, so it's important to identify the most relevant, profitable conversions for your business.

Imagine you run an armed security service. On your website, a downloadable PDF offers a detailed explanation of your security procedures. From analysis, you determine that people who download the PDF are more likely to purchase your service.

So, you bid $5 for a phone call, and $20 for a download, which assigns a greater conversion value to the download.

By tracking the conversion value metric, you can achieve a higher ROI and will continue to find opportunities for more profitable bids.

4. Cost per Acquisition (CPA)

This is how much you pay to get each conversion. The average CPA lets you see how profitable your campaigns are, or if they are no longer offering a satisfactory profit margin.

If one conversion has a value of $50, and the average CPA is $10, then it's pretty good. While some conversions may cost more, the disparity between value and cost is good enough to ignore such discrepancies.

5. Traffic Source

If you're wondering if Google Ads are working for you, look at your traffic sources. If a lot of conversions are coming from organic traffic or referrals, then you may just be throwing money away on advertising. Conversely, if most conversions come from your ads, then see how you can maximize your advertising ROI to get more bang for your buck.

6. Bounce Rate

A bounce is when a visitor lands on your page and then leaves without interacting or visiting another page.

Bounce rate = total number of bounces / total visitors

It's in your best interest to reduce your bounce rate if you want to increase conversions. Nobody will convert if they aren't hanging around long enough on your site.

7. Exit Page

This is the page users leave your site from. Keep an eye on this to find weak points in your site, as they may be proving stumbling blocks on the buyer's journey.

If users are exiting your site just before checkout, then there may be over-complicated steps that frustrate customers. It's much easier for them to leave and visit a competitor.

RETENTION

Retention marketing is a form of marketing that aims to maximize the value of customers you already have. It is the practice of engaging with customers beyond their initial purchase and making them loyal, long-term, and engaged customers.

Customer retention is when a company or product retains its customers over some specified period. Good customer retention means customers of a brand continue buying its products or availing of its services. For most industries, the average 8-week retention is below 20%. For products in the media or finance industry, an 8-week retention rate of over 25% is considered ideal. For the SaaS and e-commerce industries, over 35% retention is considered ideal.

- Benefits of Customer retention include:

- Cheaper strategy than customer acquisition

- Builds brand trust and customer loyalty

- Engaged customers are keener to provide feedback

- Engaged customers are more forgiving of any mistakes

- Easier to enable customers to review your other products

- Customer retention strategy is very useful if you want to increase your brand engagement and loyalty.

10 ways to improve customer retention on digital platforms

1. Maintaining the integrity & quality of our services:

   Any company must live up to its promises while delivering its services. Any inconsistency between what was promised and what is being delivered can hamper the brand impression.

A customer invests a lot of time and energy in making his/her decision about a particular service. Hence, there should be no gaps between the communicated benefits and the final product or experience.

2. Crafting personalized content for our audience:

   The traditional ways of making purchases and the modern ways of web-based commerce surely have one thing in common, i.e., the perspective of the customers. They are highly influenced by the way the business interacts with them – traditionally through its personnel. However, as the world moves increasingly digital, content becomes a primary way to connect with consumers. Personalized content, tailored to our customer's unique preferences can create a positive experience on our platform, by increasing their loyalty to our brand.

3. Creating user-friendly websites & mobile applications:

   The user interface of a brand platform plays a major role in user retention. If the user is encountering difficulty in going through the platform and is getting the same service on some other website much more smoothly, s/he would surely make a switch. Here, a smartly planned design can also lead to enhanced retention. For example, the addition of a chatbot function to the website helps the users in getting their issues resolved instantly. Ergo, a positive web experience is a major pillar in customer retention.

4. Uncompromising customer service:

   The experience we offer to our customers is later going to take the shape of verbal evidence regarding our brand. Simple steps like offering an immediate response, providing delivery updates, living up to the said promises, solving customers' grievances, taking feedback about the services, etc. can go a long way in building delight and loyalty.

5. **Engage and re-engage regularly:**

   Social media algorithms favour those accounts which interact regularly with their followers. It is imperative to engage with our current and former customers. Even if a customer has bought something from our platform, they don't need to contact us for their future purchases. To encourage this, we need to re-engage with him/her and persuade him/her to explore our platform for other services too.

6. **Boosting customer loyalty by dint of digital platforms:**

   They say a minor increment in the customer loyalty program can result in a major increase in profits per customer. Crafting an efficient customer loyalty program so that the customers can enjoy significant returns ensures retaining customers for a longer time.

7. **Feedback should be respected, always:**

   92% of customers read reviews on different platforms before making their final purchase. This figure highlights the importance of customer feedback and dictates how important it is for us to ask our consumers for their valuable feedback. Positive feedback will help in creating a fine influence on others and negative feedback will help us evolve. In either case, the benefit is ours!

8. **Share success:**

   Customers form our extended family and it's always great to share our success with them. Making them a part of our success story will enhance our relationship with them. Sometimes, sharing the accomplishments of one customer with all the other customers also gives rise to some new bonds.

9. **Keeping a tab on data and analytics:**

   Collecting consumer data helps us in understanding their overall behavior. It gives us detailed insights into why a customer is exhibiting loyalty and why others aren't. Tracking their usage lets us know what attracted them to make a purchase and what services didn't impress them enough. These analytics help us in understanding the overall picture as to what conduct is helping us and what activities are inhibiting our growth.

10. Regular customer engagement through SMS & Emails:

Business success relies upon multiple purchases from a particular set of customers. That's why we need to remind them of our services in different ways regularly. The two most preferred means for this purpose are SMS and Emails. People lay their hands on these two modes of communication quite often and that's why they become the most popular routes for our marketing.

PERFORMANCE EVALUATION

Once you've established the differences between Branding and Marketing, it's time to execute their respective strategies. After your campaign implementation stage, the team needs to proceed to Digital Marketing Performance Evaluation. Thus, knowing how to evaluate Digital Marketing Performance Data is critical to proving the progress or failure of a company's promotions endeavours. After all, the whole point of creating a Digital Marketing Plan is to use it to gain potential customers that are sure to convert. However, your plan is unsustainable and won't help you long-term if you can't ensure its effectiveness. You can apply a variety of channels to convert interested site visitors, such as your website, Search Engine Optimization or SEO, and Social Media. A marketing performance assessment is a means of measuring the success of a marketing campaign or ongoing marketing activity in order to determine whether they can be improved upon in the future.

Digital Marketing Evaluation for Campaign Performance:

Step 1. First, Identify and Set Your Business Objectives.

Before executing your campaign, you must first set your goals or business objectives. After all, your campaign is directionless without any endgames to achieve! Finding desired objectives can help narrow down the metrics or KPIs you want to achieve. Thus, to better evaluate Digital Marketing Performance, it's recommended to set criteria or targets for actionable items that can make up a thorough Digital Marketing plan.

Step 2. Set a Timeframe or Timeline.

Since you already have goals in mind, now you must come up with a realistic timeframe to achieve them. This can tell you how well your plan can work in that period. So consider scheduling regular meetings with your team — weekly or monthly will do. Monitoring your progress is crucial to Digital Marketing success. You need to specify the start of the campaign and set aside some time to review your progress data.

Step 3. Identify Target Segments to Focus On.

When creating your Digital Marketing campaigns, consider the audience you're marketing to. So after setting up goals and a timeframe, you must set up your target market. "74% of consumers feel frustrated" when website content isn't personalized. To get results, you have to engage with potential customers. Thus, you've got to focus on getting the attention of Qualified Traffic — that is, people interested in what you've got to say or offer. The data you collect from that traffic can then be used to improve your campaign.

Step 4. Establish Your Key Performance Indicators.

It's critical to know how your KPIs relate to the goals you set during Step 1. Also, you must know precisely what you're trying to measure, as it feeds into your final results. Thus, it's critical to figure them out and how you can achieve them in the timeframe you set. Keep in mind that the metric you're measuring should be related to the user's experience. After all, human behavior is the thing driving your Return on Investment.

Step 5. Create a Metric Map to Evaluate Digital Marketing Efforts.

Once you've found your Digital Marketing Metrics, you need to set up a Metric Map or Template. Such a guideline can be modified and scaled to your needs while providing valuable insights. Your Metric Map can include an overview of the campaign events and what worked and didn't. So, you must set specific targets that relate to your KPIs.

Step 6. Use A Good Analytics Platform for Web, SEO, and Social Media.

Part of Digital Marketing Performance Evaluation is having the right tools for the job. You'll be looking at data on various metrics. So having an analytics platform handle the bulk of the tedious work makes your work easier. There are plenty of analytics platforms to choose from, such as Google Analytics, Semrush, Hubspot, etc. These tools can work for Web, SEO, and Social Media. For example, having stagnant Social Networking accounts is one of the top Digital Marketing Challenges that's incredibly easy to fix.

Step 7. Lastly, Execute Real-Time Improvements Based on Measurement Results.

Once you've formulated the perfect Digital Marketing Strategy for your brand, now you have to put it in motion.

The essential thing about Digital Marketing is that you keep improving with every iteration of your campaigns. So, of course, you need to rely on your Digital Marketing Performance and its evaluations to find out what you can improve.

Map Out Your Digital Marketing Metrics Plan

Key Performance Indicators can be tracked with various tools, as mentioned earlier. But such indicators can be spread across multiple channels. First off, to evaluate Digital Marketing Performance, you'll need to monitor these two metrics:

Overall Website Traffic

Total ROI (Website or Social media): Equates to how much you spent (investment) vs. how much you earned (return).

Overall, KPIs can help you monitor your campaign progress towards particular goals. But, naturally, you've got to cater to the human experience or UX. So while measuring data, you still have to consider the people who make up your traffic.

For instance, Sprout social created a Social Media metrics map for each stage of their marketing funnel with sets of objectives, strategies, and different paid, earned, and owned metrics their buyers need. How they evaluate digital marketing efforts is something we can also follow.

Social Metrics Map

BUYER'S JOURNEY	OBJECTIVE	SOCIAL MEDIA STRATEGY	SOCIAL ACTIVITY	SOCIAL KPIs	BUSINESS IMPACT
AWARENESS	Create awareness	Expose target audience to brand content	Owned: Posts Earned: Influencers engaged Paid: Promotions, Boosts	Impressions, reach, cost-per-impression	SOV, ToMA
CONSIDERATION	Generate demand	Drive engagement of target audience with brand content	Owned: Posts Earned: Interactions Paid: Boosted Posts, targeted ads	# of engagements, types of engagements	Visitors/traffic (online or offline)
DECISION	Drive conversion	Move target audience to brand offers	Owned: Posts with CTAs Earned: Shared links Paid: Targeted ads with CTAs	Link clicks, cost-per-click	Conversions (purchases, leads, app downloads, etc)
ADOPTION	Delight customers	Drive engagement with brand product/services	Owned: Customer interactions Earned: Responses Paid: Promoted customer content	(Positive) Earned mentions, customer care (responses, times, qty)	Sentiment and satisfaction
ADVOCACY	Inspire evangelism	Activate customer influencers	Owned: Posts Earned: Outreach to influencers Paid: Boosted influencer posts	Earned impressions, reach, social UGC	Referrals, influencer activity, positive word of mouth, NPS

source: https://www.syntacticsinc.com/

Website KPIs that You Should Be Monitoring

- **Traffic by Source.** Monitors where your site visitors come from — whether it's search engines, advertisements, etc.

- **Mobile Traffic.** This KPI shows how many mobile users used accessed your site.

- **Page Views.** The total number of pages that a website visitor viewed.

- **Most Visited Pages.** The most valuable areas of your website.

- **New vs. Returning.** This shows how relevant your website content is over time. Thus, multiple visits can indicate you're offering content that people find so valuable that they keep coming back.

- **Sessions.** How many visits your website receives, in 30-minute increments as counted by Google.

- **Average Session Duration.** This KPI shows the average time a visitor has spent on site.

- **Exit Rate.** Reveals something about your website design and user experience.

- **Bounce Rate.** The percentage of website visitors who leave right after viewing only one webpage.

- **Conversion Rate.** It could be an actual sale, or just a new subscriber, a completed download, a lead entry, etc. Also, this metric depends on what strategy you have executed for your campaign.

SEO KPIs for Digital Marketing Performance Evaluation

- **Conversion Rate.** Indicates how many people landed on your page, completed a goal, started a trial, or bought a product.

- **Organic Traffic or Sessions.** How many visitors or sessions came from a search engine.

- **Click-Through Rate (CTR).** The ratio of searchers who clicked on your SERP results vs. the total users who only saw it.

- **Bounce Rates.** The percentage of visitors who "bounce away" without doing a particular action like clicking a link.

- **Load Time.** This metric refers to how long it takes for your website to appear.

- **Keyword/Search Rankings.** You can use this KPI to track keywords that your pages can rank with. It's key to finding the position of your website on SERPs.

- **Domain Authority (DA).** It can indicate a website's ranking.

- **Backlinks.** The number of backlinks or external pages or domains that link to your site.

- **Pageviews.** The total number of pages a website visitor views, which can indicate engagement.

- **Average Session Duration.** This metric tells you how long organic visitors stay on your site.

- **Social Media KPIs to Evaluate**

- As to Social Media or Social Networks, here are common KPIs to evaluate Digital Marketing Activities:

- **Social Reach.** This metric tells you exactly how many people saw your content.

- **Social Engagement.** The total number of interactions made on any given social media post.

- **Impressions.** This is important for clients who are running a branding campaign. For example, ads may be shown multiple times to the same person. Each time counts as an individual impression.

- **Email Open Rate.** The rate of people who open your email campaign compared to the overall number of those who received it. In other words, this metric shows the following: properly segmented list, attractive subject line, appropriate send time, etc.

- **Click-Through Rate.** Determines your relevance score.

- **Cost Per Click (CPC).** Reflects the amount you pay for each click a user performs.

- **Cost Per Conversion.** Tells you how much it costs to convert a site visitor into a sale.

- **Cost Per Acquisition or CPA.** Helps you back into the proper amount you should spend to acquire a new one, in case of returning customers.

UNIT 1 EXERCISE

1. Answer the questions in short.

- MEANING OF DIGITAL MARKETING and DIFFERENCES FROM TRADITINAL MARKETING

- TOOLS USED FOR SUCCESSFUL MARKETING

- VISIBILITY and VISITOR ENGAGEMENT

- CONVERSION PROCESS

- RETENTION

2. Answer the questions in detail.

- MEANING OF BLOGS, WEBSITES, PORTAL AND THEIR DIFFERENCES

- RETURN OF INVESTMENTS ON DIGITAL MARKETING VS TRADITIONAL MARKETING

- E-COMMERCE

- SWOT ANALYSIS OF BUSINESS FOR DIGITAL MARKETING

- PERFORMANCE EVALUATION

UNIT 2

SEARCH ENGINE OPTIMIZATION

1. ON PAGE OPTIMIZATION TECHNIQUES

2. OFF PAGE OPTIMIZATION TECHNIQUES

3. PREPARING REPORTS

4. CREATING SEARCH CAMPAIGNS

5. CREATING DISPLAY CAMPAIGNS

SOCIAL MEDIA OPTIMIZATION

1. INTRODUCTION TO SOCIAL MEDIA MARKETING

2. ADVANCED FACEBOOK MARKETING

3. WORD PRESS BLOG CREATION

4. TWITTER MARKETING

5. LINKEDIN MARKETING

6. INSTAGRAM MARKETING

7. SOCIAL MEDIA ANALYSTICAL TOOLS

SEARCH ENGINE OPTIMIZATION

"It's important to look beyond rankings and rather ensure a website is usable for everyone."

INTRODUCTION

Search engine optimization (SEO) is the process of improving the quality and quantity of website traffic to a website or a web page from search engines. The process of getting traffic from free, organic, editorial, or natural search results in search engines. It aims to improve your website's position in search results pages. Remember, the higher the website is listed, the more people will see it.

ON PAGE OPTIMIZATION TECHNIQUES

On page optimization refers to all measures that can be taken directly within the website in order to improve its position in the search rankings. on-page SEO is the practice of optimizing elements on a website in order to rank higher and earn more relevant traffic from search engines.

On-Page SEO Techniques

1. Integrate Relevant Keywords into Your Pages

2. Optimize Your Title Tag and Meta Description

3. Create User-Friendly Content

4. Optimize Images

5. Optimize Your URLs

6. Use Internal Links On Your Page

7. Improve Site Load Time

8. Add Responsive Design to Your Website

1. Integrate Relevant Keywords into Your Pages

SEO keywords are the keywords and phrases in the web content that make it possible for people to find your site via search engines. A website that is well optimized for search engines "speaks the same language" as its potential visitor base with keywords for SEO that help connect searchers to the site. Keywords are important because they help you understand what users are searching for and the content you need to provide to meet their needs. The keywords you choose help define your content strategy and what topics to include on your website. Keywords are words or phrases in the content of your web pages that match the words and phrases users are entering into search engines as closely as possible. Keywords allow you to build an SEO strategy around specific target phrases in a way that's meaningful and measurable. To integrate relevant keywords First, use your main keyword in the first couple of sentences of your content, or at least within the first paragraph. Next, use that keyword and variations of it, throughout the content.

2. Optimize Your Title Tag and Meta Description

Title tags and meta descriptions are bits of HTML code in the header of a web page. They help search engines understand the content on a page. A page's title tag and meta description are usually shown whenever that page appears in search engine results. The meta description summarizes a page's content and presents that to users in the search results. The title tag is an HTML tag that exists in the head section of each webpage. It provides an initial cue or context as to the topical subject matter of the page it is on. The title tag features prominently on search engine results pages (SERPs) as it is typically used as the clickable link and also appears in the browser window. Other than in these two places, the title tag isn't as visible as other on-page web content (e.g., body copy, image content, and other aspects). For that reason, the title tag can sometimes be overlooked. On its own, the title tag has little impact on organic rankings. No single ranking factor is magical or powerful – especially if your content is low-quality or you've neglected technical SEO. The meta description is an HTML tag (technically, it's called an HTML element) that provides search engines and searchers a summary of what a webpage is about.

It is displayed on search engine results pages (SERPs) underneath the title of the page. The URL, title, and meta description together form what is called a search snippet.

The three qualities of a valid meta description are:

- Users can type whatever text they want, without any restriction, as long as it describes what the webpage is about.

- The summary must be appropriate for use by a search engine.

- There can only be one meta description per webpage.

  Meta descriptions can help drive clicks, traffic, potential conversions, and revenue by convincing users that the webpage contains the information they are looking for. It has been considered a standard SEO best practice for years to keep meta descriptions at around 160-165 characters' maximum.

3. Create User-Friendly Content

A user-friendly website is a page that looks professional and is easy for anyone who visits your website to navigate — including those who require certain accessibility needs. Producing user-friendly content means creating text that is accessible and easy to understand. User-friendly website is visually appealing.

It's uncluttered; screens don't contain a lot of extraneous information. Important information is clear, obvious, and visible. But that doesn't mean that less-critical information is available or accessible. A user-friendly website makes it easy for users to look for information using any device. Because your website is easy to use, users spend more time interacting with your website, eventually resulting in conversions.

4. Optimize Images

Image optimization refers to the process of creating and delivering high-quality images in the right format, dimension, and resolution for whatever device is accessing them, all while keeping the smallest possible file size. The purpose of optimization is to achieve the "best" design relative to a set of prioritized criteria or constraints. These include maximizing factors such as productivity, strength, reliability, longevity, efficiency, and utilization. Image optimization is about reducing the file size of your images as much as possible without sacrificing quality so that your page load times remain low. It's also about image SEO. That is, getting your product images and decorative images to rank on Google and other image search engines.

5. Optimize Your URLs

Website optimization is the process of using controlled experimentation to improve a website's ability to drive business goals. The goal of website optimization is to drive more traffic to a website, increase your number of conversions, and ultimately, increase revenue. All too often, marketers and website owners skip to other marketing strategies without ensuring that their company's website is fully optimized. A URL consists of five parts: the scheme, subdomain, top-level domain, second-level domain, and subdirectory. URL stands for uniform resource locator. It is also referred to as an internet address, web address, or link, and is the reference that is used in a search engine to locate a web page. You can think of a URL as a house address. It gives someone looking for your address the tools they need to locate the house.

6. Use Internal Links On Your Page

An internal link is any link from one page on your website to another page on your website. Both your users and search engines use links to find content on your website. Your users use links to navigate through your site and to find the content they want to find. Search engines also use links to navigate your site. Internal links are important because they can help Google understand and rank your website better. By giving Google links to follow along with descriptive anchor text, you can indicate to Google which pages of your site are important, as well as what they are about. Internal links are hyperlinks that point to different pages on the same website. These differ from external links, which link to pages on other websites. Internal linking is when a site links to URLs located on the same domain, whereas external linking is when a site links to URLs located on other domains. Internal links help users and search engines better find pages within your site. They can help to increase rankings to other pages within your site. Links (both from other websites as well as the links within your own site) are important to SEO because there is a direct correlation between quality/quantity of links to your site and how much search traffic your site receives. For small businesses, more links = more search traffic = more customers. Links allow users to navigate a website or web application. An effective link is self-explanatory, telling the user where they will go if they click on the link. Linking Good Sources , Increases Credibility Linking to high-quality and credible sources is a good way to gain customers' trust. Always link back to your sources and don't worry about whether you'll lose traffic because of it. They may be a small detail, but their impact is definitely mighty. Social media links are external links on your website that lead to your social media pages. They play a key element in a website's link-building strategy by opening up other organic opportunities to increase your brand reach within an interested market.

7. Improve Site Load Time

The Load time is the time a website takes to show its information, I mean, the time it takes to display the entire content of a website in the browser. It is just simply a speedy website attracts more and happy visitors. Website load time — or web page load time — refers to how long it takes for a website, or web page, to fully load and appear on screen. This includes all content on the page such as text, images, and videos. Simply, it's how fast all content on a web page loads. a website's page load time is the time it takes for someone to see the content after landing. Google has indicated that website speed (and page speed) is one of the signals used by its algorithm to rank pages. The faster the pages can be loaded means Google can crawl more at one time.

8. Add Responsive Design to Your Website

Responsive web design (RWD) is a web development approach that creates dynamic changes to the appearance of a website, depending on the screen size and orientation of the device being used to view it. Responsive web design is the process of designing a mobile-friendly website that adapts depending on the visitor's device–desktop, tablet, smartphone. Responsive Web Design is about using HTML and CSS to automatically resize, hide, shrink, or enlarge, a website, to make it look good on all devices (desktops, tablets, and phones). Developers use CSS media queries to set breakpoints for each screen size so that users can browse a website within the constraints of their device. Responsive web design makes websites faster, more accessible, and easier to navigate. It makes it easier for users to them find the information they are looking for and typically encourages them to stay on your site. Plus, fantastic usability may encourage users to come back to your website in the future. A fully responsive website will rescale itself to preserve the user experience and look and feel across all devices — with no irritating zooming, scrolling or resizing. Access to content that is appropriately adapted on any device greatly improves the user experience. A good responsive design also improves readability, increases the time spent on a website, it enhances interaction or, in the case of e-commerce, improves sales. 1280×720 is considered to be the most suitable screen resolution for the desktop website version.

The 3 Major Principles of Responsive Design:

- **Fluid Grid Systems**- A fluid grid layout provides a visual way to create different layouts corresponding to devices on which the website is displayed. For example, your website is going to be viewed on desktops, tablets, and mobile phones. You can use fluid grid layouts to specify layouts for each of these devices.

- **Fluid Image Use**- Simple Fluid Images Scaling means that the image won't be cut off, but it may be large relative to text at small viewport sizes. A fluid design covers the entire browser window by specifying the width in percentages rather than pixels. When one resizes the browser or displays it at various screen resolutions, this central column will extend and contract.

- **Media Queries**- Media queries are a key part of responsive web design, as they allow you to create different layouts depending on the size of the viewport, but they can also be used to detect other things about the environment your site is running on, for example whether the user is using a touchscreen rather than a mouse. Media query is a CSS technique introduced in CSS3. Media queries are a great way to create websites that are flexible, responsive, and user-friendly. By utilizing media queries, you can optimize your website layout and content for different screen sizes, orientations, and resolutions, avoiding any horizontal scrolling or distorted images.

CSS breakpoints are used to adjust the styling of a web page to match the screen width of the device it is being viewed on. The most common breakpoints are based on the width of the device screen, but other criteria, such as screen resolution, can also be used.

5 key elements of a well-designed responsive Web site:

- Consistency. ...

- Compatibility. ...

- Whitespace. ...

- Intuitive navigation. ...

- Optimized images.

OFF PAGE OPTIMIZATION TECHNIQUES

Off-page SEO refers to SEO tactics applied outside of a website to improve its rankings. These tactics often include link building, guest posting, social media marketing, and more. The goal of off-page SEO is to get search engines (and users) to see your site as more trustworthy and authoritative.

The common off-site SEO strategies include link building, content marketing, social media marketing, guest posts, podcasting and video marketing. In short, any activity that doesn't involve publishing content on your own website falls under off-page SEO.

Some of the most important off-page SEO ranking factors include:

1. Link Authority

In SEO, authority refers to the importance or weight given to a page relative to a given search query. Modern search engines such as Google use many factors (or signals) when evaluating the authority of a webpage. In a website, a hyperlink (or link) is an item like a word or button that points to another location. When you click on a link, the link will take you to the target of the link, which may be a webpage, document or other online content.

In general, there are three types of links:

- Internal links – hyperlinks that lead from one page to another within your own website;

- External links – hyperlinks that lead from your website to another resource;

- Backlinks – hyperlinks that lead from another site to yours.

2. Anchor Text

Anchor text — or link text — is the visible, clickable text of a link. It usually appears in a different colour than the surrounding text and is often underlined. Good link text tells the reader what to expect if they click on the link.

3. Link Relevancy

Link relevance is whether or not a hyperlink back to your website comes from another website that topically makes sense for your brand. Link relevancy (or link relevance) is the relevance of your links. Your site must be linking to sites that are relevant to your business or niche. For example: If you're a bakery shop that specialises in creating bespoke cakes, you should be outreaching to other sites in your industry for outreach opportunities.

4. Social Shares

Social sharing describes when social media users broadcast web content on a social network to their connections, groups, or specific individuals. One of the primary aims of corporate social media marketing strategies is to generate brand awareness by leveraging their existing audience to share content. For example, commonly, you create a post on your social page aiming at your targeted audiences. But if your content is triggered and interesting, they share it. A lot of people connected to that customer (including friends, family, co-workers, etc.) on social media will know about that post. The more positive the social signals of a post, the greater the chance that it users will share it within and outside of social media. This can generate valuable backlinks, which in turn have a direct impact on the ranking of your website.

5. Reviews

To provide valuable feedback that you can use to improve your business operations and they also serve as marketing for the business. Buyers that conduct research about your business will usually be met with ratings and reviews as their first impressions. Ratings and reviews allow customers to share their experience with a product or service, and give it an overall star rating. Shoppers rely on this content to make more informed purchase decisions. Having many positive reviews can improve your company's social credibility and leave positive impressions on potential customers. Good reviews allow potential customers to trust your business and feel comfortable making a purchase from you because they know others have had pleasant experiences doing so.

6. Brand Mentions

Brand mentions are references to a company, brand or service online. These mentions often happen in product or service reviews, blog posts, educational content and news articles. Brand mentions can directly affect the online reputation of a brand or product. Brand mentions are online references to your brand, company, or product. These mentions show up in product reviews, blog posts, social media posts, and news articles. Brand mentions affect your brand's reputation, so it's important to monitor them and address any negative mentions ASAP. A well-placed mention increases the recognition of your business and trust in it. As your brand becomes more and more recognisable, more and more people will feel confident in engaging with what you offer.

7. Google Business Profile

Business Profile is a free tool that allows you to take charge of the way your business appears on Google Search and Maps. With your Business Profile, you can connect with customers, post updates, list your products and services, share your menu, and more. A Google Business Profile helps ensure that people find your business when looking for products and services like yours in their local area. Your Google My Business listing shows searchers where and how to visit your business. A Google Business Profile also improves your local SEO. A Google Business Profile provides you with the ability to list your business location on Google Maps and local search results. You can display important information about your business, including the opening/closing times, contact details or a link to your website.

8. Citations

Citations make your company visible on platforms where your customers search, so they will be able to find useful and accurate information for your business. They help your business rank higher in local search queries. In local search engine optimization (SEO), citations are mentions of your business's name, address, and phone number (commonly referred to as NAP) on a website that isn't your own. The purpose of SEO citations is to better assist people from a given location in finding businesses that offer the services and products they're interested in. They also factor into your SEO rankings on Google and other search engines. Here's a better look at how both of those things work.

OFF-PAGE SEO ACTIVITIES

Off-page SEO refers to SEO tactics applied outside of a website to improve its rankings. These tactics often include link building, guest posting, social media marketing, and more. The goal of off-page SEO is to get search engines (and users) to see your site as more trustworthy and authoritative.

- ### Brand Mentions

  Brand mentions are references to a company, brand or service online. These mentions often happen in product or service reviews, blog posts, educational content and news articles. Brand mentions can directly affect the online reputation of a brand or product. One of the biggest benefits of tracking brand mentions is customer feedback on products and services.

- ### Commenting

  A simple strategy to start building links back to your site while building strong relationships with people in your industry.

Comments are the medium that connects blog owners/writers and users/readers. Moreover, comments are the way that readers/users communicate with other readers/users as well as with the owner or the writers. To comment is to state your opinion or make a remark on something.

- **Forums**

A situation or meeting in which people can talk about a problem or matter especially of public interest: a forum for debate/discussion. A forum is an online discussion board where people can ask questions, share their experiences, and discuss topics of mutual interest. Forums are an excellent way to create social connections and a sense of community. They can also help you to cultivate an interest group about a particular subject. a public meeting place for open discussion. The club provides a forum for people interested in local history: a medium (such as a newspaper or online service) of open discussion or expression of ideas.

- **Influencer Outreach**

Influencer outreach is a process of building relationships with influencers. Technically, it involves sending emails or messages in social media to connect with the right influencer or creator. Outreach activities are meant to engage a large audience and to bring knowledge and expertise on a particular topic to the general public. Outreach activities can take several forms, such as school presentations, workshops, public talks and lab visits, etc. An influencer is an individual with the power to affect buying habits and decision-making of consumers due to their expertise and relationship with their audience. They have a large social media following and create content that generates significant engagement. The Influencer Marketing Specialist will manage highly visible blogger/influencer/ambassador campaigns and related events as well as develop and maintain relationships with established and emerging influencers across social and digital platforms.

- **Guest Author**

  A guest author is someone who is named as an author, but who did not contribute in a meaningful way to the design, research, analysis, or writing of a paper.

- **Social Networking**

  Social networks are websites and apps that allow users and organizations to connect, communicate, share information and form relationships. People can connect with others in the same area, families, friends, and those with the same interests. Social networking sites allow users to share ideas, digital photos and videos, posts, and to inform others about online or real-world activities and events with people within their social network. Social networking refers to using internet-based social media sites to stay connected with friends, family, colleagues, or customers. Social networking can have a social purpose, a business purpose, or both through sites like Facebook, Twitter, Instagram, and Pinterest.

Comparison Table for Advantages and Disadvantages of Social Networking

Advantages	Disadvantages
• Social network helps to connect with people around the world	• A lot of information is leaked through the social networks in public such as photos, videos, etc. that can be misused
• It gives the availability of easy and accessible communication tools	• It includes a lot of privacy concerns related to your personal data
• Live updates and news are available on social network platforms	• Cyberbullying cases has been increased
• It helps in branding and growth of business	• It could be a severe distraction for many people and become an addiction to them
• It gives a platform for entertainment and fun	• It can cause health issues such as sleep disorder

- **Social Bookmarking**

  Social bookmarking is the process of tagging a website page with a browser-based tool so that you can easily visit it again later. Instead of saving social media posts to your browser bookmarks, you can use different platforms' features to bookmark posts. Social bookmarking refers to websites that facilitate discussion and resource sharing within a rigidly tagged & organized taxonomy. Popular social bookmarking websites include Reddit, Digg and StumbleUpon. Social bookmarking sites allow users to access their bookmarks online, at any time, from any device. Social bookmarking sites are useful to marketers because users can add, annotate, and share bookmarked web pages with their team. Bookmarks can be public, private, or shared with specific groups. In a social bookmarking system, users save links to web pages that they want to remember and/or share.

These bookmarks are usually public, and can be saved privately, shared only with specified people or groups, shared only inside certain networks, or another combination of public and private domains.

PREPARING REPORTS

Digital Marketing Reporting At its core, marketing reporting is the process of measuring progress, showing value, and identifying actionable steps to improve marketing performance.

Primarily, digital marketing report needs to highlight business successes and key strategies and should contain the following sections:

1. Executive summary.

2. List of goals and objectives.

3. Marketing analysis.

4. Date comparison table for metrics.

5. List of completed actions.

6. Next steps moving forward.

7. Glossary to define key terms.

Tracking campaign performance: Campaign tracking is another of the benefits of marketing reporting. By using modern digital marketing reports to monitor the performance of your strategies, you will understand which activities were successful and which ones were not. A digital marketing report is a document created daily, monthly, or weekly to evaluate the overall performance of marketing campaigns designed to help a company's brand grow. A digital marketer creates this report based on extensive research and then distributes it to consumers, clients, and other stakeholders.

CREATING SEARCH CAMPAIGNS

Search campaigns are text ads on search results that let you reach people while they're searching on Google for the products and services you offer. It's great for driving sales, leads, or traffic to your website, as you can show your ads to people actively searching for your products and services.

A Search campaign is one campaign type available to you in Google Ads where Search ads can appear.

Types of ads on the Search Network. They include three main components — *a headline, display URL, and description text* — convincing users to click.

Apple Search Ads show above the App Store search results on both the iPhone and iPad. Text ads can also include extensions to expand your ad with additional information.

Keywords are words or phrases that are used to match your ads with the terms people are searching for.

Selecting high quality, relevant keywords for your advertising campaign can help you reach the customers you want, when you want. campaign goals are: *Increasing revenue, improving brand recognition, generating leads.* Campaigning helps to demonstrate that it is not just your organization that is concerned about the issue but also members of the public, voters and consumers. A successful campaign is one that demonstrates the concern of large numbers of the public.

CREATING DISPLAY CAMPAIGNS

Display advertising is defined as a mode of online advertising where marketers use banner ads along with other visual ad formats to advertise their product on websites, apps, or social media. Display campaigns serve visually engaging ads on the Google Display Network. The Display Network helps you reach people as they browse millions of websites, apps, and Google-owned properties (such as YouTube and Gmail). Display ads are used to generate interest, promote products and services, and keep your brand at the top of consumers' minds. Display ads also allow you to monitor and track your campaigns to reduce costs while increasing performance. Banners are the creative rectangular ad that are shown along the top, side, or bottom of a website in hopes that it will drive traffic to the advertiser's proprietary site, generate awareness, and overall brand consideration. This type of visual banner-style online advertising is a form of display advertising.

Advantages of display advertisingAwareness - you can build brand awareness and promote your products and services. Banners, square images with text, animations - these are all forms of display ads examples.

SOCIAL MEDIA OPTIMIZATION

Social Media Optimization (SMO) encourages businesses to assess, monitor, and alter their content to conform to social media best practices. All kinds of businesses prefer building their social media presence by putting content on platforms like Facebook, Instagram, Twitter, etc.

INTRODUCTION TO SOCIAL MEDIA MARKETING

Social media marketing is a process that empowers individuals to promote their websites, products, or services through online social channels and to communicate with and tap into a much larger community that may not have been available via traditional advertising channels. In 1997, the first official social media site was created by Andrew Weinreich, called Six Degrees. Social media marketing is the use of social media platforms to connect with your audience to build your brand, increase sales, and drive website traffic. the use of social media websites and platforms to promote products and services and connect with audiences. Social media marketing is the use of social media platforms and websites to promote a product or service. Although the terms e-marketing and digital marketing are still dominant in academia, social media marketing is becoming more popular for both practitioners and researchers.

ADVANCED FACEBOOK MARKETING

Facebook marketing is a platform that allows a brand to put their products and services in front of the audience and promote with the help of organic and paid means. In simple words, Facebook marketing is a practice of promoting a brand and maintaining its presence on the Facebook platform. Facebook advertising features include:

- Demographic targeting by Facebook user data on age, location, education, and interests.

- The ability to set ad budgets.

- Ad testing, in which multiple ad versions can be run simultaneously in order to compare ad designs and setup.

- Built-in ad performance measurement tools.

- The ability to advertise for your particular area—great for local businesses.

Types of Facebook Ads

- Image Ads. Image ads are among the most common types of Facebook ad that you'll come across. ...

- Video Ads. Online video ads are an increasingly popular option for businesses due to their use of implementation. ...

- Poll Ads. ...

- Carousel Ads. ...

- Slideshow Ads. ...

- Collection Ads. ...

- Instant Experiences Ads. ...

- Lead Ads.

Facebook's strategy is rapid growth, driven by multi-sided platform network effects, user monetization through advertisement and acquisition of adjacent competitors to remain the social media titan.

WORD PRESS BLOG CREATION

WordPress is a free, open-source website creation platform. On a more technical level, WordPress is a content management system (CMS) written in PHP that uses a MySQL database. In non-geek speak, WordPress is the easiest and most powerful blogging and website builder in existence today. WordPress is used by many of the biggest brands and most successful blogs in the world.

WordPress is a content management system (CMS) that allows you to host and build websites. WordPress contains plugin architecture and a template system, so you can customize any website to fit your business, blog, portfolio, or online store.

WordPress is an open source content management system that allows you to build websites on it. In fact, it is the most commonly used CMS in the world, taking up over 76.4% of CMS market share. Started in 2003, WordPress is older than both Facebook and Twitter. On a regular WordPress website, the administrator role is the most powerful user role. Users with the administrator role can add new posts, edit posts by any users, and delete those posts. Plus, they can install, edit, and delete plugins and themes.

TWITTER MARKETING

Twitter is an American social networking service and online news on which users interact and post with messages known as "tweets". Twitter is a service for friends, family, and co-workers to communicate and stay connected through the exchange of quick, frequent messages. People post Tweets, which may contain photos, videos, links, and text.

These messages are posted to your profile, sent to your followers, and are searchable on Twitter search. Twitter success rate grows faster as it provides users with the easiest way to share their thoughts, easily advertise their products and can make the public aware of what is going on across the world with the help of tweets and retweets, users type a tweet via mobile phone, keypad or computer and send them the tweets. Twitter SEO helps build brand recognition by increasing the visibility and reach of your tweets and profile. When your brand's tweets rank higher in search results for relevant keywords and phrases, they are more likely to be seen by a wider audience. To showcase their products and services to users on the Twitter platform, advertisers pay Twitter. Twitter has several types of ads that it uses to target its users and satisfy its advertisers. Twitter helps its advertisers to build brand awareness, nurture customer consideration, and drive sales and conversion. A Twitter marketing strategy is a plan centred around creating, publishing, and distributing content for your buyer personas, audience, and followers through Twitter. The goal of this type of strategy is to attract new followers and leads, boost conversions, improve brand recognition, and increase sales. Creating a Twitter marketing strategy will require you to follow the same steps you would if you were creating any other social media marketing strategy.

1. Research your buyer personas and audience

2. Create unique and engaging content

3. Organize a schedule for your posts

4. Analyse your impact and results

Using paid ads on Twitter is a great way to reach your audience in a more direct way than waiting for organic reach. They allow people to discover your profile, even if they don't follow your brand or hashtags. Only 43% of marketers are promoting their business on Twitter.

A Twitter Ads account is how you can set up, run, and analyse Promoted Ad campaigns on Twitter. Reach a wide audience: Twitter has a large user base, which could include your potential customers.

Using hashtags can help you reach an audience interested in a particular topic or in a particular location. Deliver customer service: The platform allows direct two-way communication with your customers.

LINKEDIN MARKETING

LinkedIn Ads is a paid marketing tool that offers access to LinkedIn social networks through various sponsored posts and other methods. LinkedIn Ads is a powerful marketing tool for B2B companies to build leads, online recognition, share content, and more.

As the world's largest online professional network, LinkedIn is inherently B2B-centric. It's where professional relationships are forged, careers are developed, and business is done. As a result, the platform is nearly ubiquitous as a content marketing channel for B2B marketers, and atop the social media chart. LinkedIn is a social media platform that can be used to build brand awareness and relationships with consumers.

By posting engaging content and participating in industry discussions, businesses using LinkedIn can market to potential customers and partners. The four pillars of an effective marketing organization are strategy, content, technology, and analytics.

Your updates appear directly in a follower's LinkedIn feed.

1. Use a "Follow" button on your site or blog. ...

2. Invite your Profile connections to follow your LinkedIn Page.

3. Let your employees know your most important Page posts to boost the organic reach.

4. Promote your Company Page on emails, newsletters, and blog posts.

LinkedIn ads are sold through the ad auction, where your bid competes with other advertisers who want to reach the same target audience. The target audience is made up of the LinkedIn members you're trying to reach with the ad campaign. Follower ads are a type of dynamic ad personalized to your audience. These ads promote your LinkedIn Page to others in hopes that they'll hit that follow button. Goals: Brand awareness, website visits, and engagement. LinkedIn follower ad specs: Ad description: Up to 70 characters. Many business owners are extremely successful in using LinkedIn ads to get more leads and sales.

INSTAGRAM MARKETING

Instagram marketing is a type of social media marketing, which involves promoting a brand on Instagram. This social media platform helps brands connect with an enormous audience, increase brand awareness, and boost sales. Instagram is a free photo and video sharing app available on iPhone and Android. People can upload photos or videos to our service and share them with their followers or with a select group of friends. They can also view, comment and like posts shared by their friends on Instagram. Unlike other apps, Instagram allows you to add hashtags to public stories. This makes your story visible among others when people search for a particular hashtag/location. Apps like Facebook and Twitter do not have this feature.

Build Your Instagram Marketing Strategy

1. Set your goals for Instagram.

2. Determine your Instagram target audience.

3. Conduct a competitive analysis.

4. Configure an editorial calendar.

5. Build a consistent brand on Instagram.

6. Grow your Instagram follower base.

There are four main types you may choose to employ, either individually or in conjunction with one another: organic marketing, paid content, influencer marketing, and shopping.

Instagram ads are non-intrusive and less likely to annoy your targeted audience. The engagement rate on Instagram is higher than the engagement rate on any other social media platform. You can easily integrate Shopify and sell your products instantly.

Nearly 80 percent of marketing professionals integrated the photo and video sharing app into their digital marketing campaigns in 2021.

Marketers flock to the app primarily because of its large global user base that spans audiences across many generations. Using Instagram for business can drive brand awareness, boost sales, and build and track audience engagement. It's an excellent way to find customers where they're already spending time. It can also provide valuable audience insights to use with all your marketing plan strategies. One wonderful thing about Instagram is that, even if you only have a free account, it can still be an effective marketing tool for you. Yet, if you want to pack an even harder punch, you can use the platform's advertising features as well.

SOCIAL MEDIA ANALYSTICAL TOOLS

Social media analytic tools are essential for measuring the performance of social media marketing campaigns. By leveraging a tool, businesses can make informed decisions about their social media strategies at scale, such as what content to create and when to post it.

Social media analytics tools enable businesses to track and measure important key performance indicators (KPIs) such as engagement rates, reach, and impressions. Social media analytics tools help in optimizing the strategies and eliminating the steps that are not working.

Social media analytics tools also help in analysing the regular impact of your strategies and connecting with your potential customers in a much better way. Tools that help to facilitate social media. Examples include RSS, blogs, video logs, widgets, tags, forums, location based services, Web chats, instant messaging, podcasts and microblogging services. Businesses often analyse this information to gain critical information about the interests and habits of consumers who use social media platforms frequently. This can help a company learn more about its target audience and alter its promotional content accordingly.

Conversion rates are one of the most prominent metrics most companies track because it tells you how much revenue your social media marketing is bringing in. Your conversion rate is the number of people who take some kind of action on your page divided by your page's total visitors.

There are six general types of social media metrics that should be tracked.

- Performance metrics. ...

- Audience analytics. ...

- Competitor analytics. ...

- Paid social analytics. ...

- Influencer analytics. ...

- Sentiment analysis.

UNIT 2 EXERCISE

I. Answer the questions in short.

- **Define SEO and SMO.**

- **Write a note on Social media marketing.**

- **Write about Creating search campaigns.**

- **What is Creating display campaigns?**

- **What are social media analytical tools?**

II. Answer the questions in detail.

- **Write in detail about ON PAGE OPTIMIZATION TECHNIQUES and OFF PAGE OPTIMIZATION TECHNIQUES.**

- **What is PREPARING REPORTS in SEO? write example report also.**

- **Write on WORD PRESS BLOG CREATION and LINKEDIN MARKETING.**

- **Write on TWITTER MARKETING and ADVANCED FACEBOOK MARKETING.**

- **Write on INSTAGRAM MARKETING.**

UNIT 3 SEARCH ENGINE MARKETING

1. MEANING AND USE OF SEARCH ENGINE MARKETING

2. TOOLS USED- PAY PER CLICK

3. GOOGLE AD WORDS

4. DISPLAY ADVERTISING TECHNIQUES

5. REPORT GENERATION

WEBSITE TRAFFIC ANALYSIS, AFFILIATE MARKETING AND AD DESIGNING

1. GOOGLE ANALYTICS

2. ONLINE REPUTATION MANAGEMENT

3. E-MAIL MARKETING

4. AFFILIATE MARKETING

5. UNDERSTANDING AD WORD ALGORITHM

6. ADVERTISEMENT DESIGNING

KEYWORDS- PPC, GOOGLE AD WORDS, REPORTS, SEM, GOOGLE ANALYTICS, AD DESIGN, SOCIAL MEDIA, AFFILIATE

SEARCH ENGINE MARKETING

"Nothing influences people more than a recommendation from a trusted friend."

– Mark Zuuckerberg

MEANING AND USE OF SEARCH ENGINE MARKETING

Search engine marketing (SEM) is a method of promotion and advertising to help companies' content rank higher among search engine traffic. Like search engine optimization (SEO), search engine marketing helps companies improve the way content is ranked by search engines. search engine marketing, businesses pay for their adverts to appear alongside search queries in search engines. Google, Yahoo, Safari, and Bing, for example, are search engines. A search engine is a software program that helps people find the information they are looking for online using keywords or phrases. Search engines are able to return results quickly—even with millions of websites online—by scanning the Internet continuously and indexing every page they find.

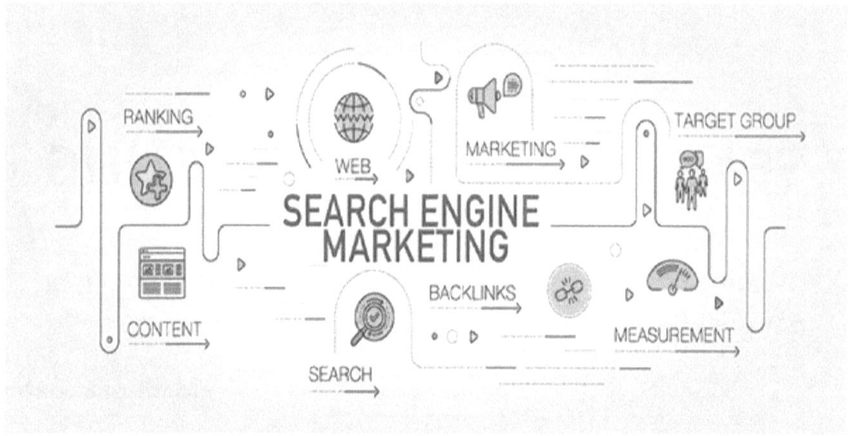

The ultimate goal of SEM is to increase your company's website visibility on search engines — and by search engines we mean Google, Yahoo, and Bing. SEM is also referred to as search marketing, and Google is the most popular search platform. Google is the most frequently used search engine worldwide.

Benefits of Search Engine Marketing

- Brand recognition. One of SEM's most significant advantages is brand recognition.

- Increased traffic. Increasing website traffic is important if you operate a website since you must wait impatiently for visitors.

- Gaining consumers' attention.

- Quick results.

- Easy to manage.

Popular examples of search engines are Google, Yahoo!, and MSN Search. Search engines utilize automated software applications (referred to as robots, bots, or spiders) that travel along the Web, following links from page to page, site to site.

Google is a fully-automated search engine that uses software known as "web crawlers" that explore the web on a regular basis to find sites to add to our index. The three main functions of a search engine are collecting information about webpages, categorizing those webpages, and creating an algorithm that makes it easy for people to find relevant web pages.

TOOLS USED- PAY PER CLICK

A PPC tool is a software application that helps businesses manage and optimize their pay-per-click (PPC) advertising campaigns. These tools can be used to automate various aspects of a campaign, such as keyword research, ad creation, bid management, and performance tracking.

The most obvious and widely used tool for PPC keyword research is Google's Keyword Planner. Pay-per-click marketing is a form of digital advertising where businesses display ads on sites like Google (paid search) and Facebook (paid social) and only pay when someone clicks on the said ad. PPC, which stands for pay-per-click, is an online advertising model where advertisers run ads on a platform such as Google Ads and pay a fee every time someone clicks on it. Run almost any search on Google (or Bing), and you will see ads displayed at the top of the results page.

CPC is calculated by dividing the total cost of clicks by the total number of clicks your ad received over a given period. It represents the amount you're willing to pay for a click on a specific marketing channel and campaign.

Major types of PPC marketing

- **Search Ads:** These appear in search results on top or bottom of your search engine page, typically labeled with the word 'ad' to indicate that they are sponsored. According to Google, search ads are capable of boosting brand awareness by 80 percent.

- **Display Ads:** These are targeted ads that show up on partner sites and are focused on people who have visited similar websites to your own. Display ads combine image and text for maximum appeal.

- **Social Ads:** All those sponsored posts you come across on social networking platforms like Facebook, Twitter, LinkedIn, etc. are social advertisements. Social media sites offer advanced targeting based on location, demographics, behavior, education, interests, etc.

- **Shopping ads:** These PPC ads are presented in a carousel format on search engines like Google. They let you see the product and prices from different companies before you visit a particular website, providing you with a window-shopping feel.

- **Email ads:** Sponsored promotions on email services such as Gmail are another excellent way of reaching your potential customers. Users receive these ads based on their interests, demographics, etc.

Essential PPC tools for professional digital marketers

1. Ads Editors

Formerly known as Google Adwords, Google Ad Editor comes with all the necessary features for bulk edits and optimization for massive ad campaigns. This PPC management tool lets you work across multiple accounts and is a must-have in your toolkit. For managing campaigns on Bing, you can use the Bing Ads Editor, which is an all-in-one tool.

2. Google Ads Performance Grader

It is an excellent auditing tool that grades your ads based on more than sixty factors, including ad spend, click-through rates, account activity, quality score, etc. You can get an instant report on your PPC metrics to help you improve your digital marketing efforts or just to justify to your management why you are investing in Google Ads.

3. WordStream Advisor

This tool has been specifically designed for small to medium-sized organizations. It helps you maximize your returns from online advertising by providing feedback on critical performance aspects.

WordStream is a time-saving software and also has a free trial of their basic platform.

4. AdEspresso

It is an ad management and optimization tool for Facebook and Instagram advertisers.

5. Google Keyword Planner

Google Keyword Planner is an indispensable means of getting ideas and traffic estimates. It helps you search for the most suitable and competitive keywords for your online ad based on your product, service, category, website, etc. It also tells you how many impressions or clicks your keywords might get.

6. Google Trends

PPC marketers consult this tool for adjusting their campaigns to meet seasonal demand. Using this data source is free and proves immensely valuable while executing search network campaigns. The Google Trends website compares the search volumes of different search queries over time and presents the information in the form of graphs.

7. SpyFu

Originally called GoogSpy, SpyFu exhibits those keywords that websites appear for in Google search results. It also lists the keywords that websites are buying on Google Ads.

8. SEMrush

It is another competitive research tool that services detailed keywords and domain data. SEMRush helps boost SEO by tracking the keywords used by your competitors and running an audit of your blog or site.

9. iSpionage

iSpionage a monitoring platform or an intelligence tool that provides meaningful SEO data. It sizes up the online marketing efforts of your competing websites and assists you in generating more leads and bringing in targeted traffic to your business forum.

10. Invoca

Phone calls are an important source of business leads. And PPC tools like Invoca help you capture and manage calls. It is an AI-powered platform that supports marketers in gaining actionable insights from inbound calls.

11. CallRail

This tool allows you to track, record, and analyze phone calls. Also, CallRail features can be easily integrated with Google Ads and Google Analytics.

12. Twilio

Staying connected to your customers is a breeze with cloud communication platforms such as Twilio. You can buy local or toll-free numbers, make and receive phone calls, and also record these calls. Besides facilitating voice calls, its API lets you send text messages, emails, and even WhatsApp messages.

13. BuzzSumo

Amid increasing digital clutter, making your PPC advertising catchy and clickable holds prime importance. BuzzSumo gives you article headlines and ad keywords by scanning what people are talking about on social sites. It is, thus, a powerful online tool for inspiring your ad copy.

14. Answer The Public

Copywriters need to use the language of their prospects when they are trying to answer questions. Keyword tools like Answer

The Public visualize search queries and surface the problems of your target audience, ensuring that your ad content addresses their needs as closely as possible.

15. Canva

Canva is a popular online tool for creating display ads and graphics. Its drag-and-drop interface and most of its layouts come free of cost, except for some paid library images and features. You can also design striking social media posts using this visual resource.

16. Share as Image

It is an online graphic design tool with which you can turn text into images within seconds. You can make micro-content, add text and logos to any image, and create impressive display ads.

17. Pinterest

As a digital marketer, finding appealing for visual content can sometimes seem challenging. With platforms like Pinterest, you can access 'mood boards' and find inspiration for your online ads. You can discover, organize, and save moving images and visuals that match your story, messaging, and project objectives.

18. Gifntext

As the name suggests, gifntext can be used to create GIFs for social or display ads. You can generate emotive visuals and creative animated images to catch the attention of easily-distracted audiences and hence, drive click-through rates.

19. Facebook Text Overlay Tool

Facebook and Instagram have a rule that the images or video thumbnails of your display ads should not contain text beyond 20 percent. Facebook Text Overlay ensures that you meet this requirement.

20. Leadpages

A landing page is a web page where visitors are directed upon clicking on your PPC ad. The Leadpages tool provides various templates to put together stunning landing pages. Additionally, it enables lead generation and comes with built-in analytics.

21. Unbounce

It is another landing page tool that contains stencils for constructing attractive sites. The drag-and-drop builder makes it easy to learn and develop internet advertising campaigns at scale.

22. Twitter Analytics

Twitter has an activity dashboard where you can go through the metrics of every Tweet. The Twitter Analytics tool tells you whether your campaign is working by informing you about what people are seeing and engaging with, what demographic do your followers fall in, among other things.

23. Google Analytics App

This mobile application makes possible on-the-go monitoring of statistics and reports. You can use it for measuring how your PPC ad efforts are translating in the real world and what you can do to improve your reach.

24. Google Ads App

Some of the features include keyword bid adjustment and Google Ads object modification (such as specific ads, campaigns, ad groups, etc.). The Google Ads Script tool, you can automate the time-consuming tasks like variant matching and competitor tracking with your Google Ads account.

25. Facebook Ads Manager App

This mobile application equips you to undertake the functions of performance measurement, ad editing, budget adjustment, and even new ad creation on Facebook. So, it is no surprise that this Ad

Manager App is being used by more than 800,000 online advertisers each month.

PPC advertising has emerged as one of the most lucrative marketing channels today. Social Media Today reports that 40 percent of brands want to boost their PPC budget. In order to get the most out of your campaign, you should aim for a high 'quality score.' This score highlights the rating of your ad content. And the higher the ratings, the lower are the costs that you bear per click.

GOOGLE AD WORDS

AdWords is Google's PPC advertising platform and main source of revenue. Typically, PPC advertisers use AdWords to bid on the keywords they want to trigger their sponsored ads.

Google launched AdWords in 2000 .Google Ads (formerly Google AdWords) is an online advertising platform developed by Google, where advertisers bid to display brief advertisements, service offerings, product listings, or videos to web users. It can place ads both in the results of search engines like Google Search (the Google Search Network) and on non-search websites, mobile apps, and videos. Services are offered under a pay-per-click (PPC) pricing model. Google Ads is the main source of revenue for Alphabet Inc, contributing US$168.6 billion in 2020.

Features

Advertisers manage ads on the Google Ads website or using *Google Ads Editor*, a downloadable program that allows users to make bulk changes to ads and edit ads offline.

- The *Keyword Planner* provides data on Google searches and other resources to help plan advertising campaigns.

- *Google Ads Manager Accounts* (previously "My Client Centre (MCC)") allows users to manage multiple accounts from one login and dashboard. This is most commonly used by Marketing and Advertising agencies who manage a large portfolio of client accounts.

- The *Reach Planner* allows users to forecast the reach and extent of their video ads across YouTube and Google video partners. The tool allows users to choose their audience, then recommends a combination of video ads that help reach the user's objectives and see the reach of their ads.

- In addition to location and language targeting, advertisers can specify Internet Protocol (IP) addresses to be excluded. Advertisers can exclude up to 500 IP address ranges per campaign.

- *Placement-targeted advertisements* (formerly Site-Targeted Advertisements) places adverts based on keywords, domain names, topics, and demographic targeting preferences entered by the advertiser. If domain names are targeted, Google also provides a list of related sites for placement. Advertisers bid on a cost-per-impression (CPI/CPM) or cost-per-click (CPC) basis for site targeting.

- *Remarketing* allows marketers to show advertisements to users that have previously visited their website and allows marketers to create different audience lists based on the behavior of website visitors. Remarketing Lists for Search (RLSA) via Google Analytics became available in Google Ads in early June 2015, allowing for the use of standard GA remarketing lists to plan traditional text search ads. Dynamic remarketing can show past visitors the specific products or services they viewed. While common, some users may find overly overt use intrusive.

- *Ad extensions* allow advertisers to show extra information with their ads, such as a business address, phone number, links to a web page or app, prices, or sales and promotions. Google Ads may also display automated extensions such as consumer ratings when the system predicts they will improve performance.

- The *Performance Max* type of campaign, is used to run a single campaign across multiple Google channels such as YouTube, Display, Search, Discover, Gmail, and Maps, instead of having to create one for each channel.

DISPLAY ADVERTISING TECHNIQUES

Display advertising appears on third-party websites and uses video, image, or text elements to market products or services. Display advertising campaigns can be run through advertising networks such as Facebook advertising or Google ads that provide powerful audience targeting features as well as advertising formats (that you can also combine with search ads).

Types of display ads

Display ads vary greatly in terms of who they target and how they work. Here's a breakdown of the different display ad options and what they do.

1. Remarketing ads

Most display ads you see today are remarketing ads, also known as retargeting ads. Thanks to the trend toward ad personalization, retargeting campaigns have become widespread.

According to Accenture Interactive, 91% of consumers prefer to buy from brands that remember their interests and provide offers based on their needs. Retargeting ads do just that, and they're easy for brands to implement. Here's how they work.

- To start, place a small section of code onto your website that collects information about visitors' browsing behavior, including when they navigate to a category or product page.

- From the information you collect, develop lists of customer types and what kinds of advertising messages would most likely appeal to them.

- Then create and place display ads based on the different categories of interest you have observed.

A dynamic remarketing campaign is an effective way to keep your brand present in the minds of shoppers who have already shown interest in what you have to offer.

2. Personalized ads

Google considers remarketing to be a subcategory of personalized advertising, which can be effective when you segment your audience to deliver a better user experience. Personalized ads target consumers based on demographic targeting and the interests they have shown online. You can even create ads that show personalized product recommendations based on a user's recent interactions with your website.

In addition to remarketing, Google recognizes 4 distinct types of personalized ads. Each incorporates general user behavior and preferences rather than interactions with any particular brand as a targeting option.

Affinity targeting

Affinity targeting shows your ads to consumers who have demonstrated an active interest in your market. These affinity groups can be relatively broad—like "car enthusiasts" or "movie lovers"—letting you reach large numbers of people.

Custom affinity groups

Smaller custom affinity groups like "long-distance runners" and "orchid growers" let you get more specific about the interests you want to target. Bear in mind that when you use narrower groups, you'll reach smaller audiences.

Custom intent and in-market ads

Custom intent and in-market ads target consumers who are actively searching for products or services like yours. You'll reach fewer people than with either affinity or custom affinity targeting, but the people who do see your ad will be closer to making a purchase.

Similar audience ads

Similar audience ads target people who have interests or characteristics in common with your current visitors. To create lists of new but similar audiences, Google compares the profiles of people on your remarketing lists with those of other users, then identifies commonalities.

3. **Contextually targeted ads**

   Instead of displaying your ads to people based on their user profiles, contextually targeted ads are placed on websites according to certain criteria, including:

   - Your ad's topic and keywords

   - Your language and location preferences

   - The host website's overarching theme

   - The browsing histories of the website's recent visitors

4. **Site-placed ads**

   If you'd prefer to hand-pick the websites that will host your ad, website placement targeting is your best bet. You can select entire sites or individual pages within sites. You can even combine placement targeting with contextual targeting. With this approach, you choose a site and let Google select the most relevant pages for your ad.

How to measure display ad performance?

In order to properly allocate resources and run a successful campaign, you must determine the effectiveness of your display ads. Whether you're using Google Ads or another platform, you can track campaign performance throughout the entire campaign and make adjustments where necessary. There are a few key metrics to keep an eye on when measuring your campaign, including:

- **Impressions**: Impressions are the number of times your ad was displayed on a website. Your campaign impressions should grow over the life of your advertising campaign, as this proves you're reaching a wider audience.

- **Reach**: People often get impressions and reach confused. Reach is the number of individuals who saw the ad, while impressions measure the times your ad appeared on a website.

- **Cost**: You should always have a budget for your advertising campaign and measure cost to determine different ways to reduce costs while improving other metrics. You can measure the total cost of running the campaign, cost per click (CPC), or cost per thousand impressions (CPM). Display advertising typically uses the CPM measurement.

- **Click-through rate (CTR)**: The number of clicks your ad generates divided by the number of impressions is the CTR. CTRs are displayed as percentages that represent how much of your audience clicked on your display ads.

- **Conversion rate**: The main goal of advertising is to convert. Conversion rate is the percentage of individuals that converted from the ad. Depending on your campaign, you might have more than one conversion action, whether it's having a customer purchase a product or sign up for a mailing list. The conversion rate describes the lead conversion rate when your display ad is used to generate leads.

BEST PRACTICES FOR DISPLAY ADS

Be respectful of your audience's experience

Avoid autoplay video ads, pop-ups, and any ads that your viewers can't get rid of by scrolling away. These tactics will certainly get people to notice you, but not in the way you'd like. Instead, try placing a static ad near the edge of the screen or within the site's text. Another rule of thumb is to make sure that your ad doesn't cover more than one-third of the screen. High ad density can irritate users by blocking the content they came to see, especially if they're on mobile devices.

Use a simple design

Your brand story is important, but display ads are often too small to include every detail. To avoid overwhelming users, stick with a simple design and use as few words as you can to get your message across.

Go for quality over quantity

Because you're only including the essentials, make sure everything looks good. Use high-resolution images, easily readable type, and a logo that's clear and bold. Remember to preview every image after you export it.

Include a strong call to action

Your call to action, or CTA, is the most important part of your display ad. An effective CTA will encourage users to click through to your site's homepage, a specific product page, or a special promotion.

It can be tempting to create a simple CTA like "click here" or "continue," but getting specific will make it much more effective. Here are some tips for creating a strong CTA.

- **Make your CTA benefit-oriented**. CTAs like "Download Our Free eBook" or "Find Out More" let viewers know that they'll receive something of value if they click through.

- **Use persuasive language**. Entice your viewers with promotional items or potential discounts.

- **Create urgency**. Convince your audience that they'll lose out if they navigate away from your ad.

- **Make the button the focus**. Your CTA button shouldn't just be easy to find; it should be impossible to miss.

REPORT GENERATION

Marketing reporting is the process of gathering and analysing marketing data to create a clear report.

The goal is to inform future marketing decisions, strategies, and performance. Great digital marketing reports uncover meaningful, actionable insights and inspire action.

Report generation refers to the process of extracting the data that you need from the database and then organizing and exporting them into reports.

It provides decision-makers with informative insights and supportive references. A report generator is a computer program whose purpose is to take data from a source such as a database, XML stream or a spreadsheet, and use it to produce a document in a format which satisfies a particular human readership.

Reports will provide important detail that can be used to help develop future forecasts, marketing plans, guide budget planning and improve decision-making.

7 Practical Ways Generated Reports Will Benefit Your Business

- Ensures Accuracy. ...

- No More Time-Squandering Process. ...

- Saves Money Considerably. ...

- Less Time Spent on Initiation Training. ...

- Easy Storage and Access.

- Better Collaboration with Clients. ...

- Robust Security and Confidentiality Maintained.

The report generation module allows you to directly extract all the information you want from the database and either view it directly online or export it in open formats. This second possibility makes it possible to take back the data and their formatting by means of external spreadsheets.

GOOGLE ANALYTICS

Google Analytics is a web analytics service that provides statistics and basic analytical tools for search engine optimization (SEO) and marketing purposes. The service is part of the Google Marketing Platform and is available for free to anyone with a Google account.

Google Analytics for marketers Audience helps you explore who your customers are, including information such as demographics, location, retention, and device technology. With these metrics, you can interpret the impact of your marketing efforts on various user segments. Google Analytics is a platform that collects data from your websites and apps to create reports that provide insights into your business. Google Analytics is a very important tool for website owners, as it provides valuable insights into how users are interacting with their digital assets and marketing campaigns. This information can be used to improve the user experience, increase website traffic, and ultimately drive more sales and revenue. Real-Time Reporting. Monitor activity on your site or app as it happens.

- Acquisition Reports. ...

- Engagement Reports. ...

- Monetization Reports. ...

- Data Freshness (Analytics 360 Only) ...

- Sub-Properties (Analytics 360 Only) ...

- Roll-Up Reporting (Analytics 360 Only)

Google Data Studio is a Google Data Analytics tool for Reporting Metrics and Data Visualization.

It allows you to easily analyze page view, session and bounce rate for multiple websites. Google Analytics provides a great overview with bar charts and graphs to know the number of user visits, their engagement, geographic area, etc. It can be integrated with Google Console and Adword tool easily to manage data.

ONLINE REPUTATION MANAGEMENT

Online reputation management is a practice of structuring a brand's reputation on the internet by displacing misleading content, uploading trending content, and making it visible through the help of other internet algorithms. For a user, the brand must display or provide correct solutions for their queries.

STEPS TO BUILD AND MANAGE YOUR ONLINE REPUTATION:

- Decide how you want users to see you.

- Evaluate your current online reputation.

- Design a social media policy.

- Design a social media content strategy.

- Post quality content.

- Engage with your audience.

- Monitor your online reputation.

Reputation management in digital marketing is the practice of monitoring and managing a brand's image using online tactics.

Reputation monitoring allows digital marketing agencies to get a strong grasp of how current and potential customers view a brand.

Other key metrics that can measure your online reputation include:

- Leads or referrals from review sites.

- Overall customer sentiment.

- Website traffic from social media platforms and organic search.

Manage Negative Feedback. Brands getting negative feedback lose their reputation, resulting in declining sales and profitability. Online reputation management enables you to fix issues before they get out of hand. This means making necessary adjustments to products and services and ensuring customer satisfaction.

An online reputation, or e-reputation, is the reputation of a company, person, product, service or any other element on the Internet and digital platforms.

A reputation management strategy is a process of managing a person's, company's, or brand's online narrative. It is part of monitoring views and conversations, dealing with reputation threats, and proactively taking opportunities to improve brand image.

Reputation management refers to the efforts a business makes to take ownership of their online reputation. It is essentially the actions, content, and damage control a company adopts to influence what and how people think about their brand. Reputation management is categorized into two types: proactive and reactive. Three phases of online reputation management: Building your online reputation. Maintaining your online reputation. Recovering your online reputation. The dimensions of the company's online corporate reputation are "quality," "pleasantness," "innovativeness," "reliability," "responsibility" and "successfulness."

Objectives of Brand Reputation Management

- Get More Customer Feedback.

- Connect with Your Customers On Social Media.

- Promote Your CSR Strategy.

A negative online reputation can lead to negative word-of-mouth, with customers sharing their negative experiences with others. This can damage the business's reputation further and reduce the chances of making a sale to new customers.

Reputation management is controlling and influencing the audience's perception of the brand through responding to customer feedback. Companies use social media monitoring tactics and reports from a customer care team to analyze reputation. They manage reputation through social media, emails and chatbots.

E-MAIL MARKETING

Email marketing is the act of sending a commercial message, typically to a group of people, using email. In its broadest sense, every email sent to a potential or current customer could be considered email marketing. It involves using email to send advertisements, request business, or solicit sales or donations. Email marketing is a type of direct digital marketing method that uses emails to engage with a business's audiences. It involves sending promotional or informational content. Email marketing is typically used to create product or brand awareness and generate leads or sales.

Examples include postcards with an offer, catalogues that display goods, coupons, solicitation letters from non-profits or free samples sent by businesses. A business or organization sends thousands of pieces of mail, hoping to get a large enough response to pay for the mailing and costs of goods sold, leaving a profit.

Emails can be used to generate sales, enhance customer engagement (i.e., newsletters), acquire customers, create brand awareness and reward customer loyalty. Email marketing is up to 40 times more effective than social media, according to a study done by McKinsey & Company.

AFFILIATE MARKETING

Affiliate marketing is the process of making money online every time a customer purchases a product based on your recommendation. This is an online sales tactic that allows you – 'the affiliate' – to earn a commission and helps the product owner increase sales.

Affiliate marketing is the process by which an affiliate earns a commission for marketing another person's or company's products. The affiliate simply searches for a product they enjoy, then promotes that product and earns a piece of the profit from each sale they make.

Affiliate marketing is a revenue-sharing marketing model in which brands deploy affiliates, such as bloggers, YouTubers, influencers, etc., to promote their products or services online. In turn, affiliates earn a percentage of the sales.

Affiliate marketing can be highly profitable for marketers who are able to build an audience and promote products that align with their interests.

With the rise of micro-influencers, even accounts with less than 2,000 followers can become great affiliates. However, a good number is 5,000 to 15,000 followers to expect a substantial sale from affiliate marketing. At the end of the day, look for high engagement rate vs. the number of followers.

The challenges of affiliate marketing include the difficulty of finding quality products and services to promote, the need to build a large and engaged audience, and the need to continually adapt to changes in the market and the products and services being promoted.

UNDERSTANDING AD WORD ALGORITHM

A mathematical calculation that uses a range of various factors to ultimately confirm your ad position.

The algorithms are Google's own mathematical calculations that use a variety of factors to confirm your final ad position (which will determine when and where your ads are shown on a specific page and for specific audiences).

The ad rank determines your ad position. The ad rank determines whether or not your ad is eligible to appear with ad extensions, site links etc. Here advertiser-1's ad won't rank as his keyword's quality score is very poor (1).

The Quality Score is the key to running Google AdWords. The Quality Score is typically the relationship between ad group, keywords, ad and landing page and what a person is looking for and the likelihood that someone will click on the ad. Here's the Google page for "Quality Score, Review and Understand."

Clickthrough rate is an important measure to better understand the results of online marketing campaigns.

The CTR helps us to better understand the number of visitors to our websites online as a result of a campaign.

To Calculate CTR We Divide the number of clicks through to the site divided by the number of total impressions. Then we multiply it by 100.

For Example: if your Ad has 1000 impression and 20 clicks then your Ad will have CTR of 1%

CTR 2% $= 20/1000 \times 100$

CTR is an important parameter for ad analytics because it gives you an idea of how your keywords and ads performing.

The percentage of clicks is important as it directly affects the quality score. Google is interested in the overall user experience and rewards advertisers with the most relevant ads.

A high CTR means a higher quality score, which means higher ad placement and lower cost-per-click. So what is the right CTR?

In general, you must aim for at least 2%. However, a good CTR is different for each keyword.

In your account, Google gives estimates as to whether your CTRs are good, bad, or average, so you can monitor them closely.

Ads are sorted by ranking. The highest Ad Rank wins first place, and so on, until the last bid that is valid for the auction or the last position on the page.

Ad Rank = Quality Score * Bid

What the advertiser actually pays is the lowest amount needed to outperform the competitors below him.

How, much each advertiser competes because of its rankings Again a slightly simplified version.

This is called an "AdWords Discounter" and there are few questions related to this on each certification exam are intended to understand the following.

In many ways , understanding this information is the key to completely unlocking AdWords.

$ = Quality Score + $0.01.

Understandin g AdWords Algorithm (Adrank) in detail with examples

Let's put this into practice using real-life examples, and I'll show what I mean by the importance of *Quality Score (QS)*.

Goa+beach+house +for +sale has a QS = 8

Let's say we want to be first on the page, no matter what. We cannot guarantee that, but we can certainly be pretty sure if we go beyond the keyword and say $80.

Ad Rank = 640= (QS 8 * $80 Bid)

To win, a competitor must have an Ad Rank> 640. This means that even with a QS 8 keyword, he has to bid $ 80.01 per click to get the first place.

Assuming that you have a more realistic offer of $10/ click, the amount we would pay at the auction will be calculated as follows.

Ad Rank to beat = 80 = (QS 8 * $10 Bid)

$10.01 = 80 / 8 + $0.01 = (80 Ad Rank to beat / our QS 8 + $0.01)

So even though we bid $80, we only pay $10.

If our Quality Score on that keyword in that auction was 8, then the amount we would pay is:

$9.98.00 = 80 / 8+ $0.01 = (80 Ad Rank to beat / our QS 8 + $0.01)

It's going to be really interesting here. The person in the first place could pay less than the people among them.

Sounds Crazy? This is the reason why this happens. Assuming the same $ 80bid for first place, let's say that the next participant has only a 4 QS keyword for a $ 10 bid, and next person has QS 6 in a $ 6 bid and the person in position 4 has the keyword QS 7 in a 9 dollar bid.

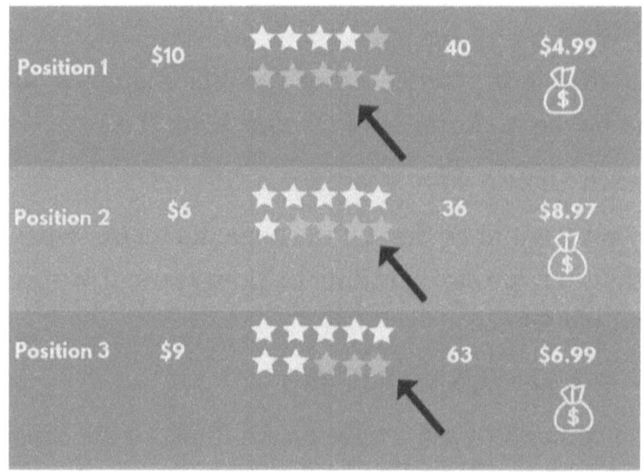

Position 1:

Ad Rank

40 = (QS 4 * $10 Bid)

$4.99 = 40 / 8 + $0.01 (40 Ad Rank to beat our QS 8 + $0.01)

Position 2:

Ad Rank to beat = 36 = (QS 6 * $6 Bid)

$8.97 = 36 / 4 + $0.01 (36 Ad Rank to beat / #2 QS 4 + $0.01)

Position 3:

Ad Rank to beat = 63 = (QS 7 * $9 Bid)

$6.99 = 63 / 9 + $0.01 (63 Ad Rank to beat / #3 QS 7 + $0.01)

In this example, our keyword QS 8 in position 1 reports less than positions 2 and 3.

This calculation applies regardless of the position displayed so that the person in position 3 can pay less than position 4 immediately

If you have a keyword of quality 10, you control the bid.

With a Quality 10 keyword, you know that not only will you pay the least amount for the work you do, but you'll have to ALL over you be forced to pay the PLUS.

They cannot defeat you unless you defeat them.

In the past, we used this to force a competitor to leave a keyword, especially if he bought a branded keyword that we knew was the highest quality level (and conversion rate).

It's great fun to stay in position 2 and slowly increase the quotes with a QS10 keyword, as the automated systems at the other end only increase the bids and costs for the competitor.

In the meantime, we have paid only the minimum amount that should be displayed in the auction as there was no other competitor. You do not pay ten times more than you do per click.

ADVERTISEMENT DESIGNING

"Advertising Design is the voice of a brand. It's everything you see through multimedia, traditional or interactive media. It's everything from television, print advertising and mobile applications that you're interacting with on a daily basis."

Online advertising, also known as online marketing, Internet advertising, digital advertising or web advertising, is a form of marketing and advertising which uses the Internet to promote products and services to audiences and platform users.

The main advantage of digital marketing is that a targeted audience can be reached in a cost-effective and measurable way. Other digital marketing advantages include increasing brand loyalty and driving online sales.

Graphic designers represent their designs in two main mediums: images and type. Within advertising, graphic designers use information such as the needs of the client, intended message portrayed by design, and appeal to customers or users before creating a new design.

Good graphic design will help a business to gain high visibility which in turn can lead to increased sales. Attractive visuals, effective communication of ideas, higher visibility and enhanced credibility push traffic to your brand. Increased traffic leads to more opportunities.

Designing an ad is a multi-step process that takes time and effort. The main steps are target audience research, deciding the budget, creating copy, adding visuals, and testing. Based on your needs, additions can be made to these steps.

Digital marketing helps marketers to get deeper insights into customer behavior, tastes, and preferences. This helps in creating better print advertisements to attract customers and increase engagement.

Digital Marketers: Digital Designers focus on creating the best experience for a specific person (or avatar) who will interact with the design. Digital Marketers focus on using digital solutions to get the greatest number of people to interact with the design.

Digital advertising refers to marketing through online channels, such as websites, streaming content, and more. Digital ads span media formats, including text, image, audio, and video.

There are four core channels of digital advertising: search, display, social, and video.

Measuring user engagement is one of the most common ways of tracking success in digital marketing. It makes sense: by measuring how users engage with your online activities, you get direct metrics about the people you are targeting. That's important to every marketer.

- Click-Through Rate(CTR)

The CTR measures the number of users that click on your ads. Set a goal to have a higher CTR than the industry standard. CTR ensures that the message and the journey for your prospects from your ads to the landing page are optimized.

UNIT 3 EXERCISE

I. Answer the questions in short.

- Meaning and use of search engine marketing
- Online reputation management
- Advertisement designing
- Report generation
- Display advertising techniques

II. Answer the questions in detail.

- Tools used- pay per click
- Google ad words and ad word algorithm
- Google analytics
- E-mail marketing
- Affiliate marketing

CASE STUDIES ON DIGITAL MARKETING

A case study in marketing is an in-depth examination of a specific marketing campaign or strategy, with the goal of providing valuable insights into the approach's success or failure. It is a detailed examination of a real-life marketing scenario, usually focusing on a specific product, service, brand, or organization.

Cases are taken from existing secondary data available on internet developed by professionals and educators for knowledge purposes. As an author I would like to give credit and thanks to all the bloggers, professionals and educators for their deep research and hard work which is helpful for aspiring candidates.

Source: Google search, Blogs, case studies from linkedin, company resources, study material etc.

CASE 1

JOBRAPIDO MORE THAN TRIPLED ITS ORGANIC TRAFFIC THOUGH THE JOB EXPERIENCE ON GOOGLE SEARCH

About Jobrapido

Jobrapido is one of the global leaders for job search engines with more than 20 million unique job postings every month and more than 80 million registered users. Being present in 58 countries, Jobrapido's mission is to revolutionize the way people get jobs.

Easy to integrate

Jobrapido decided to integrate with the job experience on Google Search to attract more motivated applicants: "We know that job seeking is a struggle and as a technology company, it is our duty to improve it the best way we can, with minimum effort for job seekers. Jobrapido has always been one of the first companies to adopt Google's new services with the goal to constantly improve the user experience", says Jean-Pierre Rabbath, Jobrapido VP of Product. "In fact, adding the job markup for us was really easy and allowed us to get the best of the job experience on Google Search rather quickly".

Increased international traffic

Jobrapido has seen positive metrics and feedback from job seekers on their site across multiple geographies. In all countries, the company's overall organic traffic grew by 182%, and they have seen a 395% increase in new user registrations from organic traffic since launch of the new job experience on Google Search. Jobrapido also noted a 35% drop in user bounce rate, which means the quality of the end user journey also increased.

182%	395%	35%
Increase in organic traffic	Increase of new user registrations from organic traffic since launch of the new job experience on Google Search	Lower bounce rate for Google visitors to job pages

CASE 2

LARGE IMAGES IN DISCOVER IMPROVE CTR AND INCREASE VISITS TO PUBLISHER SITES

"In 2020, we gave publishers more control over how images from their site appear in Discover with the introduction of the robots `meta` tag `max-image-preview` setting. When added to the header of each site page, the `max-image-preview: large` `meta` tag indicates that Google can feature publishers' images in large formats, creating a more compelling and engaging user experience when their content appears on Search surfaces, like Discover.

Since the introduction of this tag, we're excited to see the success of web publishers who have reported greater visibility of their content within Discover including increased clicks and traffic to their site as well as improved click-through-rate (CTR)." a statement by an entrepreneur.

CASE 3

DilHaiHindustani Hashtag Campaign by MakeMyTrip

Make My Trip is a high-quality travel agency that is also well-known on social media channels. All students should follow this brand since they are always presenting innovative campaigns and deals, particularly during the holidays. By rewinding the revolutionary efforts for freedom, the online travel business exploited Independence Day as a key event to reach the youth.

They created the **#DilHaiHindustani**, which depicted India's freedom journey from 1857 to 1947. The Mangal Pandey agitation, the Jallianwala Bagh massacre, the non-cooperation movement, Chandra Sekhar's Kakori railway theft, and others were all mentioned.

People may participate by picking their favourite freedom fighter in the blog, sharing the blog by noting the name of the freedom fighter and the cause and increasing their chances of winning prizes by using the hashtag **#DilHaiHindustani.**

CASE 4

IPL Team's Digital Marketing Strategy by KKR

Even the Indian Premier League club couldn't avoid the digital world. Kolkata Knight Riders (KKR) is a Twenty20 cricket franchise that represents Kolkata in the Indian Premier League (IPL). It is co-owned by Shahrukh Khan, a well-known Bollywood actor. Due to its digital marketing efforts, the KKR squad has the highest level of engagement with its fans and followers. During the early days, KKR showed a keen interest in gaining internet followers and worked on a number of objectives, including how to increase KKR brand awareness without mentioning Shahrukh Khan, how to stay tuned and connected with fans, and how to keep them up to date with the updates and latest news. To increase fan interaction, they initially chose to launch "Inside KKR," a video blog dedicated just to KKR supporters, where fans can readily access news and their favourite players. Second, they had a website blog as well as an official mobile app that kept supporters involved and informed about the team's current happenings. They devoted special attention to social media channels, and KKR's digital marketing team even hosted a live screen Facebook discussion in Facebook's Hyderabad headquarters. KKR players held Twitter chats with their supporters and ran a unique "Cheer for KKR" campaign. This is for when any sports team adopts a digital strategy.

The campaign's outcomes include:

- KKR is the most active IPL team on Twitter.
- With over 466K Instagram followers, KKR has become the most followed IPL team.

- KKR's Facebook page had more than 15 million likes during the season, the most of any IPL franchise.

CASE 5

Transferkar Family by Tata Sky

The promotion was mainly aimed at families, as the name suggests. Obviously, the campaign's goal was to promote Tata Sky's Tata Sky+ Transfer product/service. This innovative tool transmits recorded video from a television to a mobile device or a tablet computer.

Basically, when it comes to channels, everyone in each household has their own tastes. However, for some reason, not everyone in the family watches their favourite shows at the same time.

This is particularly prevalent in Indian homes, where the head of the family controls the TV remote, and the rest of the family just follows his or her preferences.

The campaign was a great hit and went viral on social media and television advertising. During the promotion, consumers were offered cheap discounts on a variety of family-related materials. The campaign was a big success because of its grasp of the intended market, becoming one of the practical and best e-Commerce Digital Marketing Case studies in India.

CASE 6

'Mom's Touch' By Nivea India

This campaign was created particularly for Mother's Day to honour all the amazing and selfless moms. Nivea's Mom's Touch ad included some incredible, altruistic mother tales from throughout the country.

The campaign was to assist moms who face a variety of challenges on a daily basis. Despite extraordinary circumstances, the woman does not give up on providing a stable future for her kid. NIVEA's Mom's Touch is a social effort aimed at assisting moms who face difficulty on a daily basis. Mothers who, despite overwhelming obstacles, will stop at nothing to ensure their children's future. By publishing this film on social media channels, the brand urged the public to share the unselfish act of their moms. Their marketing plan also had a lovely goal of increasing viewing. The brand promised that if this video were shared on social media, the brand would donate to the girls. This campaign was one of the most emotional and heart-touching e-commerce digital marketing case studies in India and was indeed a great success.

CASE 7

FloatABoat campaign by Paper Boat

Paper Boat is a well-known Indian brand of traditional beverages known for cocktails, including aam panna, golgappe ka pani, Jamun Kala khatta, and kokum, which can all be made at home. These tastes are popular among Indian families, although not everyone can make them at home. According to Paper Boat's objective, the goal of these beverages was to transport you back to those memories and float a boot this monsoon. The team also does an excellent job of carrying out the same goal through digital marketing initiatives. They devised a number of creative advertisements that appealed to the audience's emotions and made them fall in love with the brand. As the name suggests, the firm urged individuals to construct a paper boat as they did as children and post it on social media with the hashtag **#FloatABoat** and by following their social media sites.

According to the firm, Paper Boat will give Rs.20 to children's education whenever this is shared on any social media platform. The campaign's goal reached millions of people, and it was a huge success, with paper boats clogging up timelines. You can now see how many people followed Paper Boat during the campaign.

The campaign's outcomes include:

- By the middle of July, 231 boats had been posted to the site.

- The company intends to release many more versions, at least 25 in all.

- The brand is currently accessible in 20,000 retail locations worldwide, including coffee shops like Barista Lavazza, airlines like Indigo and Jet Airways, and hotels like Westin and Trident.

- In just 5 months, the videos on YouTube have received over 40 thousand views, and the emotional impact has remained with a huge number of viewers.

- The Paper Boat donations will benefit Parivaar Ashram's roughly 805 youngsters.

CASE 8

The Great Indian Freedom Sale by Amazon India

You can't overlook e-commerce enterprises when it comes to digital marketing strategies. During the same Independence Day celebrations, Amazon India, the world's largest online retailer, used new marketing methods such as product advertisements and deals and judicious use of social media. The campaign we've been discussing may serve as an excellent example of internet marketing efforts, particularly in the e-commerce industry.

The tournament was held as part of Amazon India's The Great Indian Freedom Sale, which included entertaining activities, and the winner received Amazon India shopping cards. The campaign was dubbed **#10KeBaadKarenge**, and it encouraged consumers to postpone their buying plans until after August 10th due to an Amazon deal.

Even their background, if you look at Amazon's digital marketing case studies, we can see that they have always been intelligent and witty, which has resulted in increased engagement rates and brand exposure.

CASE 9

WohEkBaat by Shaadi.com

On Valentine's Day 2019, shaadi.com ran a campaign called **#WohEkBaat** in which couples from all over the web came forward to share their one thing in common, and many TV star couples participated in the campaign, including Gurmeet and Debian, Suyyash and Kishwer, who asked their fans to share their **#WohEkBaat** on shaadi.com's social media handles.

Shaadi.com is India's most popular matrimonial website for wedding planning and social networking. It began in India in 1997 and has now expanded to include more than seven nations, including the United States, Pakistan, the United Arab Emirates, and the United Kingdom as of 2019.

The campaign's outcomes include:

- The contests had over 500 submissions on Valentine's Day, and around 200k people interacted with **#WohEkBaat** postings.

- On Valentine's Day, **#wohekbaat** achieved 1.4 million Instagram followers, an increase of 5% across all social channels.

CASE 10

Cadbury's Dairy Milk Team Digital Marketing Strategy

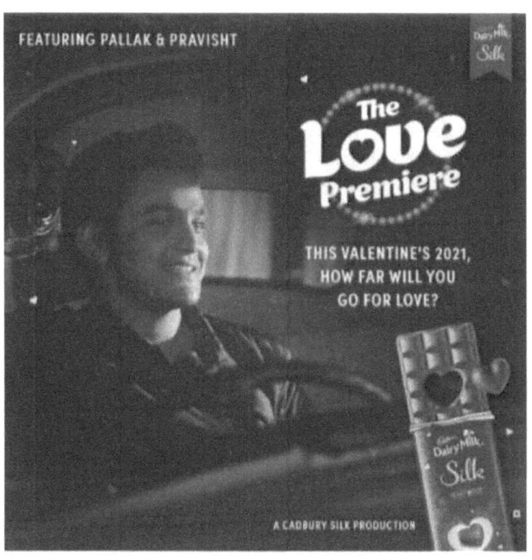

The case study will give a brief on the strategies of dairy milk silk and Spotify releases mixtapes to advertise it in various forms. How you can send the message of love with the playlists that are personalized for you.

Why they got need to advertise the dairy milk silk. This Ad was necessary for the couples who were separated by the unseen enemy; Covid 19. Dairy milk and Spotify reach out to GenZ with new strategies.

The strategy was implemented via Spotify. It applies the digital marketing experience for dairy milk silk by using Spotify's API. The users that are listening to the music have been experiencing the creative content of dairy milk silk Ads and music as well. Leisurely, the users get engagement and allow users to get a special playlist to share the file.

CASE 11

Dove – Connecting with their target audience

Is it just me or do all the Dove marketing campaigns make you cry? If you've seen their Real Beauty sketches campaign, you'll know what I'm talking about. Dove's goal is to make women feel good about themselves. They know their target market and create content that tells a story that women can relate to.

Dove did some research and found that 80 percent of women came across negative chatter on social media. Dove's goal was to change that and make social media a more positive experience. As a result, Dove teamed up with Twitter and built a tool to launch the #SpeakBeautiful Effect, that breaks down which body- related words people use the most and when negative chatter appears during the day.

According to Dove, women were inspired by their message.

- #SpeakBeautiful was used more than 168,000 times

- Drove 800 million social media impressions of the campaign

Dove know their audience. Knowing your audience is the only way you will engage with them. The best way for this is creating personas. Knowing what life stage they are in, if they're employed, what their interests are etc. will certainly help you when creating content. Then think about linking your audience to your brand values in order to create something just as successful as Dove's campaign.

CASE 12

Oreo – Smart content planning and timely delivery

Oreo is another brand that is known for their creative social media marketing. They must have a big design team to produce their content, but it works! They are consistent with their branding and manage to catch onto real time events. We all remember when the lights went out at the Super Bowl and during the half hour blackout Oreo tweeted out:

CASE 13

Gillette: "We Believe: The Best Men Can Be"

In January 2019, Gillette launched a social media campaign aiming at a modern interpretation of manhood.

The short film posted exclusively on YouTube depicted several cases of men struggling with traditional masculinity that Gillette itself used to glorify: the fear of showing their emotions, sexual harassment, and bullying others.

Then the film shows several examples of positive masculinity, such as standing up for others, caring for your loved ones, and so on.

The campaign was clearly inspired by the #MeToo movement.

On their Instagram, the company also posted positive male role models with short stories about their journey in the world:

- Organizers.

- Community leaders.

- Non-profits' CEOs.

In addition to that, the company promised to donate "$1 million per year for the next three years to non-profit organizations executing the most interesting and impactful programs designed to help men of all ages achieve their personal best."

The Numbers:

- The short film that launched the campaign has over 30 million views.

- The #GilletteAd hashtag reached more than 150 million people in one month, according to Awario (disclosure: I work for Awario), a social listening tool.

- The Instagram posts related to the campaign gathered around 800 likes and 50 comments, which is higher than usual for Gillette.

Why Did It Work?

This campaign managed to tap into an extremely relevant and widely discussed issue.

It juxtaposed the previous branding of Gillette with a new one and showed the willingness to change. At the same time, it was also quite controversial – some people didn't agree with how the short film portrayed men and thought that it was offensive.

They even started a #boycottgillette hashtag. However, it only took up around 3.5% of all the conversations around the campaign on social media. In addition to that, the company promised to donate "$1 million per year for the next three years to non-profit organizations executing the most interesting and impactful programs designed to help men of all ages achieve their personal best."

CASE 14

Starbucks U.K.: #WhatsYourName

Campaign Outline:

Starbucks U.K. partnered with Mermaids, an organization to support transgender and gender-diverse youth, for a #WhatsYourName campaign focused on trans rights.

The campaign builds on a well-known aspect of the Starbucks experience – having your name written on the side of your cup – by committing to respect the names that customers want to be called by.

In addition to that, Starbucks started selling a mermaid tail cookie to raise funds for Mermaids.

Social media users were encouraged to use the hashtag on Instagram to tell about their experience with gender.

The Numbers:

- The YouTube ad gathered 605,000+ views (with less than a thousand YouTube subscribers).

- The Instagram post gathered 1,000+ comments, with an average comment rate for the Starbucks U.K. Instagram profile being around 40 comments.

Why Did It Work?

The team behind the campaign created a simple, clear campaign hashtag and they led with their values, which helped this campaign make a real, emotional impact. Many brands avoid politicized topics, but ultimately, your employees and customers want you to take a stand. Specifically, they want companies to lead on issues of diversity and community.

CASE 15

WENDY'S: USING HUMOR TO CONNECT WITH CUSTOMERS

Wendy's Twitter Humor is basically the godfather of all funny brand social media campaigns. Almost every single fast-food chain started doing it now. But Wendy's is by far the most memorable and the funniest. Their unique and often edgy jokes help engage followers, gain recognition and foster customer loyalty. They use their platform to make people laugh while taking digs at their competitors like McDonald's or Burger King. In addition, their lighthearted approach to content can make a lasting impression on consumers, putting them at the forefront of the competition. Here are just some of the funny tweets we found from Wendy's:

CASE 16

MCDONALD'S: LEVERAGING USER-GENERATED CONTENT

McDonald's ran a campaign that encouraged customers to submit pictures of themselves at one of its restaurants in exchange for a chance to win free food.

CASE 17

COCA-COLA: CREATING CUSTOM HASHTAGS

Coca-Cola developed custom hashtags like #ShareACoke and #TasteTheFeeling, which have been used worldwide by millions of people who enjoy their beverages or want to express support for the company through these designated terms. The hashtags helped build recognizable brands that increased awareness among potential customers, making them more likely to pick Coca-Cola over other beverage options when shopping.

CASE 18

Amazon: "Aur Dikhao"

Top e-commerce players in India are Amazon, Flipkart, Indiarush, Jabong, American Swan, Vistaprint, Trendin, Askmebazaar, Paytm, and Webnexus. They offer a wide variety of products in various categories such as apparels, electronics, beauty products, fragrances, home accessories, jewelleries, among others. {Source: **Digital Marketing: Case Studies in India** by Rajendra Nargundkar and Romi Sainy}

About the Company

Amazon (Amazon.com) has emerged as the world's largest online retailer and a prominent cloud services provider. The company started its business by selling books but has extended its basket by offering a wide range of consumer goods and digital media as well as its own electronic[1]devices, such as the Kindle e-book reader, Kindle Fire tablet and the Fire Stick for TV, which is a media streaming adapter for online content. Amazon was officially launched in India in June 2013, but it now stands as the country's fastest growing e-commerce giant in terms of sales.

In the year 2015, Amazon launched the Aur Dikhao Campaign, which had the following major objectives:

1. First, to drive the message that Amazon has over 22 million products for the consumers to choose from. Having studied the typical Indian consumer behaviour, this campaign was mirrored to reverberate the desire of "what more" in the consumer. With the increasing online shoppers, the thrust for more and more options before buying a product has sky rocketed.

2. Secondly, the main objective behind the campaign was to be able to penetrate deeper into tier 2 and tier 3 cities and make amazon accessible to the masses.

3. The third objective was to engage the existing consumers, get new buyers and create a buzz around the campaign. The campaign was taken to a bigger level by creating engagement to various social media sites to attract new buyers and suppliers as well.

It offers a wide range of products, ranging from innerwear to gourmet foods. To showcase its products, it has come up with a catchy jingle ad, i.e. "Hindustani dil kehta hai aur dikhao," to make sure that it reaches the mass.es This idea has been extended well on social media with meaningful engagement and creative visuals. Connecting with Twitter influencers and creating a social buzz around #Aur Dikhao has given a good start to the campaign. The campaign was able to capture a lot of interest through the ads and videos uploaded on YouTube which got more than 21 lakh views in mere eight months. The catchy tune stuck in the heads of the viewers. Through Twitter contests, people participation increased significantly, they followed the campaign and the #Aur Dikhao with interest and creative tweets. With this campaign, the seller base steadily increased. The main reason for this was that Amazon was offering self-registration by vendors on their official websites. Today the base has increased to approximately 6500. The total net sales have increased by 300 percent compared to the same period last year. The number of units sold has also increased by 500 percent.

Times Now has stated that, given that it is a new entrant in the market, Amazon has become the most visited e - commerce site way above its competitors. {Source:Livemint.com, Business Standard, Amazon.in, wikipedia.com, youtube.com & Twitter}

CASE 19

DIGITAL MARKETING CAMPAIGNS FOR POLITICIANS IN INDIA

When Donald J Trump became the 45th president of the United States of America, one of the first statements that he gave was "social media help me win."

How can **digital marketing for political campaigns** influence voting decisions in voters?

1. Micro-targeting:

Digital Marketing for political parties has the power to reach out to the most fragmented sections of audiences and elusive voters. As a politician, you can easily make a youth connection by making engaging personalized content across all platforms. Social media allows political candidates to build their brand in their own way and engage with their voters directly.

Engagement with voters is a very important part of digital marketing campaigns for politicians. These conversations can be then tailored into relevant messages which become resonant with the voters' views and opinions.

2. Audiences:

There will be 3 major audiences that political parties can target using digital marketing strategies.

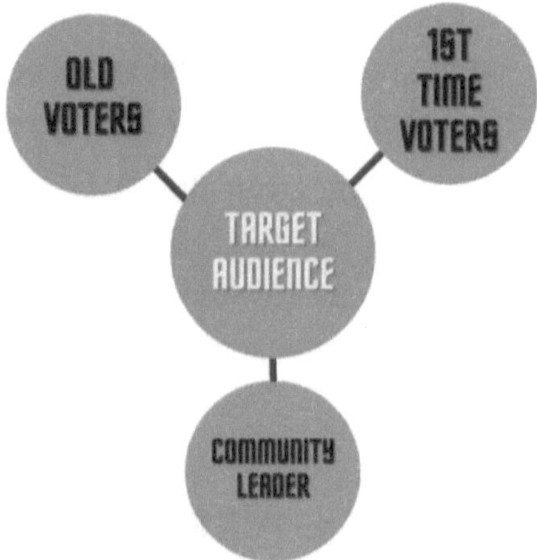

- **First-time voters:**

These are the young boys and girls who have just turned 18 and are going to vote for the first time. These are high tech-savvy individuals who spend a lot of time on social media. So digital marketing campaigns for political parties should have robust social media plans to target these individuals.

- **Regular Voters:**

They are the people who have voted earlier. They will be looking for better policy changes and will dig deeper intro reforms and earlier performances. To target these people, political parties must be very precise about the content they are making to target.

- **Community Leaders:**

  They are the influencers with a massive following among a particular group of individuals. They are looking for anything of the benefit to their community. Political parties can target them and attract their attention by posting content of their interest on the various channels. This will very much turn the odds in their favour.

3. Engaging the youth:

It is the most easily persuaded section of the society which is supposedly apolitical and is always glued to digital marketing channels. Youth are the most active and opinionated bunch of voters out there. Therefor connecting to youth should be the top strategy when it comes to **digital marketing for political parties.** Political parties can target youth in their preferable domain and mould them according to their agenda.

4. Analysing the data:

You might have heard of this saying that data is the new oil. We create an abundance of data doing our day to day activities over the internet. This data is then used by analysers to predict our behavior. Politicians can use this data and insights to mould the voters as per their agenda. Using this data, they devise various **digital marketing strategies for political campaigns.** Here's a case study of BJP's digital marketing campaigns that helped them win 2019 General Elections. **Example video link: https://youtu.be/MqKpWk5nRqc**

5. Authentication:

In the day and age of one-click shares and WhatsApp forwards, fake news and misleading campaigns can make or break the future of a political party facing the elections. There may be fake accounts spreading rumours about your party with the malicious intent of harming your political campaigns. Therefore, a politician or the political party must reach to its voters before anyone else. They should have verified accounts where they put out well thought out posts and content regarding the political campaigns that really put forward their brand.

6. Pages:

Creating your social media page is an essential step in the process that is often overlooked. A political personality's personal Facebook account will not be sufficient. Setting up a page dedicated to your campaign allows you the opportunity to run ads and give access to multiple administrators. They may post, respond to messages, or run ads on your behalf. Not only does this take some of the weight off of your shoulders, but it keeps your personal account and password safe.

7. Live Video:

Today, politics is playing out in online streaming. Between Twitter, live streaming, and 24/7 news coverage, the internet is the place we go to stay informed on political happenings. In fact, eighty-two percent of viewers say they prefer seeing a live stream over social media posts. In another poll, data shows that eighty percent of people would rather watch live video than read a blog. So digital marketing campaigns for politicians must and should include regular live streaming.

8. Polls:

One of the most interesting features that digital marketing platforms provide which can be useful for any political party is the poll feature. There are various social media platforms that provide the poll features which politicians can use when they are about to make any policy decisions. It is very different from the opinion or exit polls conducted by various market research organizations. Polls on social media can help you find out the exact insights of what your voters actually want.

9. Digital Advertising:

Digital advertising platforms like Facebook and Instagram can allow you to reach your target group of audience at a very low cost. The advertisement post generally has sponsored written over it, but generally, people overlook it when you are providing any information of some sort. A digital advertising campaign has the power to reach a large number of people as the inbuilt algorithms of these platforms help your political party to reach your exact target audience. Politicians and political parties using **digital marketing for political campaigns in India** is not a new phenomenon but the use of social media in their campaigns has definitely increased. We have seen this not only in Trump's political campaign but also in Narendra Modi's campaign, Britain's conservative party's campaign, and many more. And results have always been in their favour. All these tell that political parties looking to reach out to their target audience, digital targeting cannot be ignored.

CASE 20

FLIPKART

Flipkart is an E-commerce website, founded by Sachin Bansal and Binny Bansal in 2007. When Flipkart was launched, initially the aim was to sell books before expanding into other product categories such as consumer electronics, fashion, home essentials & groceries, and lifestyle products. In March 2017, Flipkart held a 39.5% market share of India's e-commerce industry. In August 2018, U.S.-based retail chain Walmart acquired an 81% controlling stake in Flipkart for US $ 16 billion, valuing it at $20 billion.

Flipkart is India's answer to Amazon. Flipkart is one of the most visited E-Commerce Websites and just like Amazon, the company has rapidly become one of India's original unicorns. The company is now owned by Walmart and is one of India's huge success stories.

FLIPKART'S OVERALL MARKETING STRATEGY

Flipkart's leading marketing strategy focuses on every single touchpoint their customers are present at. It uses the majority of its budget on various digital channels involving both paid and organic marketing. Moreover, since India has recently experienced digital transformation, the efforts of Flipkart are paying off.

Flipkart also invests intensely in celebrity endorsement and influencer marketing. India is crazy over Bollywood and Flipkart uses this to raise awareness about their brand and to market their services. Ranbir Kapoor, Alia Bhatt, Varun Dhawan and Shraddha Kapoor have all been brand ambassadors who were predominantly featured in Flipkart's commercials and digital marketing campaigns.

A CASE STUDY ON FLIPKART'S DIGITAL MARKETING STRATEGY

Flipkart is considered to be one of the best platforms for online shopping. Either we talk about some gadgets or apparel, Flipkart has always shown up their best quality service. Flipkart has mainly grown its business through digital marketing strategy. Let's discuss, what strategy do they follow? How do they convert their one time customers to loyal customers? How does Flipkart manage to increase the number of its customers? This article will help in the analysis of the tools used by Flipkart in their Digital Marketing Strategy.

TARGET AUDIENCE

Flipkart targets anybody who surfs the internet and who does not have time for shopping. Though it's target audience is scattered over various market segments as consumers from all demographic backgrounds can find products that appeal to their interest, 75% of its audience is between the age group of 16 – 55.

It lays focus on people seeking variety and who prefer to experience a hassle-free shopping approach from home. It tries to expand its services to every location in the country where deliveries are possible. It comes up with smart marketing strategies to seize the attention of its audience who hold the purchasing power, to influence that online shopping is better than traditional shopping.

Search Engine Optimization

Flipkart being the largest online retailer in India has worked immensely on optimizing its platform to rank on the search engine. Every time someone searches for a product, Flipkart appears among the top 2 results, and it is all possible because Flipkart has put a lot of effort into

SEO. As per Uber suggest, a keyword tool by Neil Patel, Flipkart has monthly organic traffic of 3,90,246,762 and a strong domain authority of 90.

Keywords in URL

Flipkart checks the top searches of people, it then takes the top keywords and creates web page URLs for them. This is a very good strategy for Flipkart to make sure its website ranks.

Backlinks of Flipkart

The domain has a total of 66,547,531 backlinks, these stats are really amazing. Flipkart gets backlinks from over 66 million unique domains, which is simply amazing. All these backlinks work as a backbone for Flipkart in ranking number 1 on the search engine.

Backlinks for Flipkart have increased rapidly over time. The graph below shows how from December 2019 to August 2020, backlinks have grown from 73.3 million to 98.7 million.

Site Speed

Another important aspect of Search engine optimization is Site speed. Site speed is crucial to your SEO health. Every additional 0.5s it takes to load your site drastically increases the % of visitors that will leave your site.

Keywords on the web pages

Keywords that include products' names and phrases like 'Best price' tell the search engines that these pages have the content related to these search queries.

Flipkart's Social Media Strategy

Flipkart is very much active on all social media platforms. As of August 2020, Flipkart has –

-93,96,244 followers on Facebook,

-1.7 Million followers on Instagram,

-2.4 Million followers on Twitter.

When it comes to Instagram, Flipkart has several accounts for different things, like a proper account dedicated to Tech, Clothing, and others. When it comes to businesses, be it for a product or different services, the key highlight point for the customers is Feedback and Customer Reviews. Flipkart has given special attention to that by having a separate account which just focuses on Customer Story named as FlipkartStories

Collaborations & Celebrity Marketing

Flipkart is known for its collaborations. It also invests heavily in star power and celebrity marketing. Flipkart keeps collaborating with various famous figures from time to time. One of the notable and more recent collaborations being with Ranbir Kapoor & Alia Bhatt on "#IndiaKaFashionCapital."

Under this campaign, the company invites fashion enthusiasts from all over the country to upgrade their style with the latest trends from Flipkart. Via a meaningful media mix, using styled fashion quotient and targeted communication towards their consumers, Flipkart Fashion's brand ambassadors, Ranbir and Alia, educate consumers about always being ahead in their style game by 'Wearing The Next.' The pair were seen in a variety of engaging and interactive formats, ranging from short digital content to traditional TVCs discussing the benefits of shopping on Flipkart Fashion.

CAMPAIGNS

Frequently Bought Together

Flipkart loves to understand and study customer behaviour and keeping that in mind they have started a series of 'Frequently Bought Together'. In this, Flipkart, based on the customer behaviour and purchase pattern, shares the items which are frequently bought by the audience from the app.

Don't you think it's a great way to market other products by having a psychological effect, where they tell you to opt for other products?

Flipkart Kidults

A discussion on the marketing strategy of Flipkart is incomplete without the mention of their campaign Kidults. It was launched way back in 2014 and it's yet to end. Well, that itself speaks about the success of this campaign. Right? The reason behind such an impressive track record is the refreshing concept where Kids act like adults.

Twitter Strategy

You'll be surprised to know that out of all the platforms Flipkart pays special attention to Twitter. Flipkart is known to follow a fixed pattern for communication for all the platforms but when it comes to Twitter, they keep running mini-campaigns from time to time like #SareeTwitter

Apart from fun campaigns, Flipkart has 24*7 available Customer Support System on Twitter where they address complaints and queries of their customers. Next time you face a problem with Flipkart, you know what to do.

Campaign – #Flip Girl

Flipkart launched a new campaign featuring actor Alia in the role of a 'FlipGirl' superhero to convey the ease of shopping and trust for customers. The campaign aimed to highlight the brand's commitment to making premium brands accessible through faster delivery and establishing itself as the go-to destination for online shopping.

Campaign – #MultiPurposePurchase

When it comes to merging two products or telling how to fully utilise a product, Flipkart is a master at it. Check this out

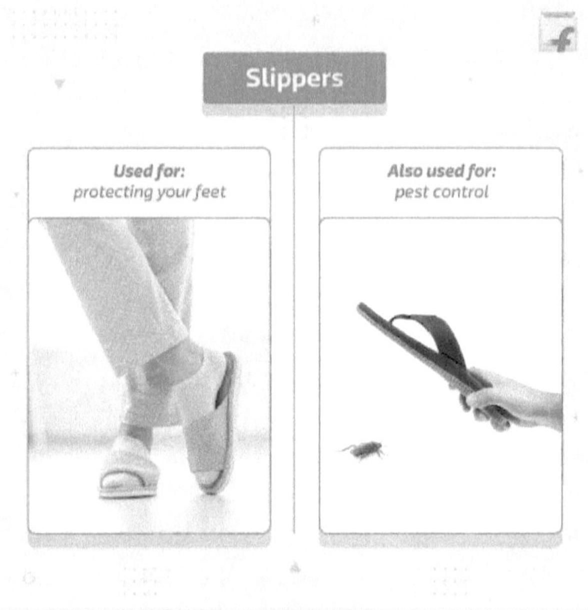

Special Occasions

The brand follows a Social Media Calendar and makes the most of the Special Days, right from universally celebrated occasions like Father's Day, Sleep Day to days of national importance like Gandhi Jayanti and Independence Day. Usually, e-commerce platforms like Flipkart and Amazon have special discounts and offers on such occasions, so these posts are not there to drive traffic but to maintain a social media presence and act as a reminder to shop.

Flipkart's VR Campaign

We all are stepping into the world of artificial reality and virtual reality slowly and we have already seen the impact and use of filters by brands for Instagram Stories. Flipkart is always up and ready when it comes to adapting to new technologies. Flipkart discovered the right opportunity to make the most of VR technology by adding it to the Big Billion Sale Campaign. No doubt that Big Billion Day campaign has massively contributed to Flipkart's marketing success and they were able to attain the goal much effectively with the advanced VR technology. The campaign was launched when Full Moon day was nearing as it is viewed auspiciously and closely associated with the festive calendar in India. Their ad campaign ran on days when there was no full moon, but Flipkart privileged its users to see a full moon shaded by clouds. Gamification prompted the users to blow into the microphone to move the clouds away revealing both the full moon and an exciting new offer. This campaign was like something never experienced before and it left the audience thrilled and excited, earning Flipkart 5 million views and a CTR of 2 %

Fun Engagement Activities

Flipkart keeps their audience engaged with different types of fun activities and with that being said they don't forget to mix it up with something which is trending. For example, during this lockdown many things have gone viral and trended, one such thing was Dalgona Coffee, remember? This is what Flipkart did

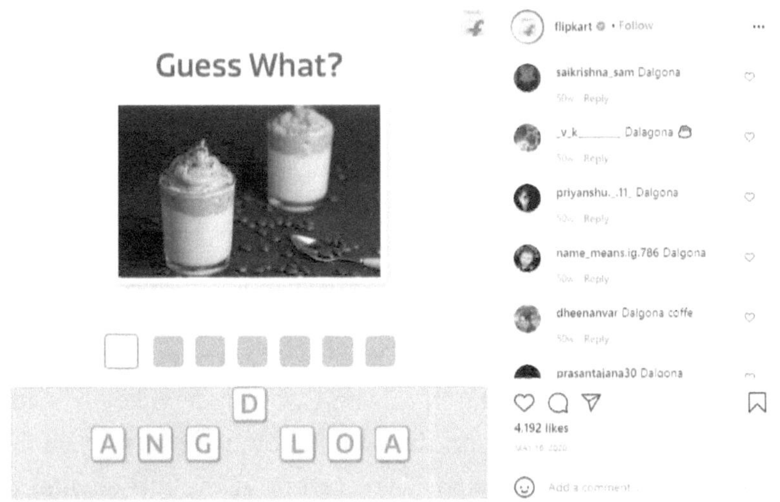

Apart from these, Flipkart is not behind when it comes to Current Affair. This is what Flipkart did during the Pride Month. With months of lockdown and everyone in their house, there was desperate need of

trimmer, see what Flipkart had to say about it. During the lockdown, the online delivery rate was on the rise, but at the same time safety was a concern, considering that the brand delivered a perfect message for No-Contact Delivery.

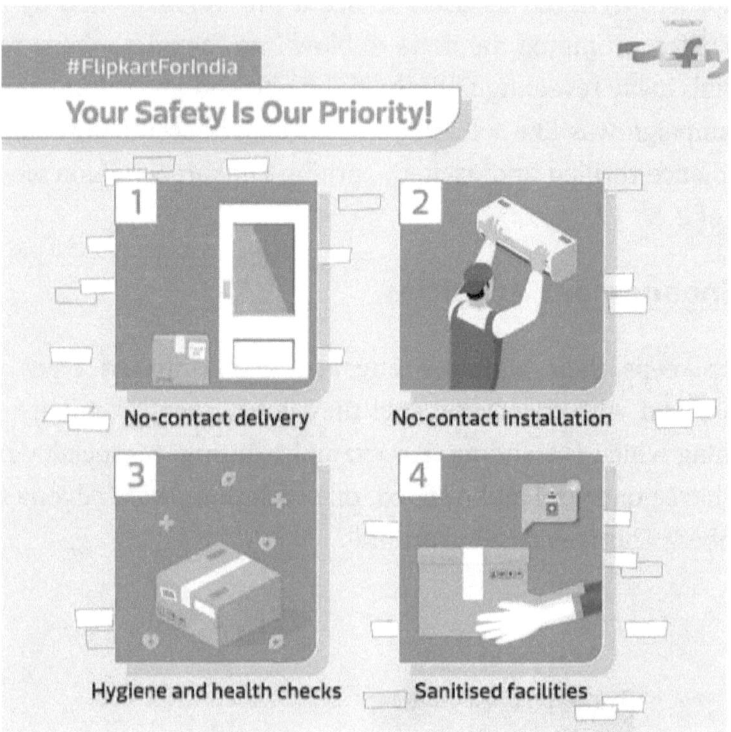

Paid Advertising

Google Adwords

When it comes to Search Ads, Google Adwords is the go-to option. Being an e-commerce platform, Search Ads on Google play a key role in both sales and bringing in traffic on the site. Today users just go on Google and search for the product and if you're not in the top results, you're missing out. Thus, Google Ads are a must. Flipkart runs display, search and shop ads the most, by carefully studying and targeting the right set of keywords. Here's an example of how Flipkart is running ads on google for random searches and driving traffic and a potential customer.

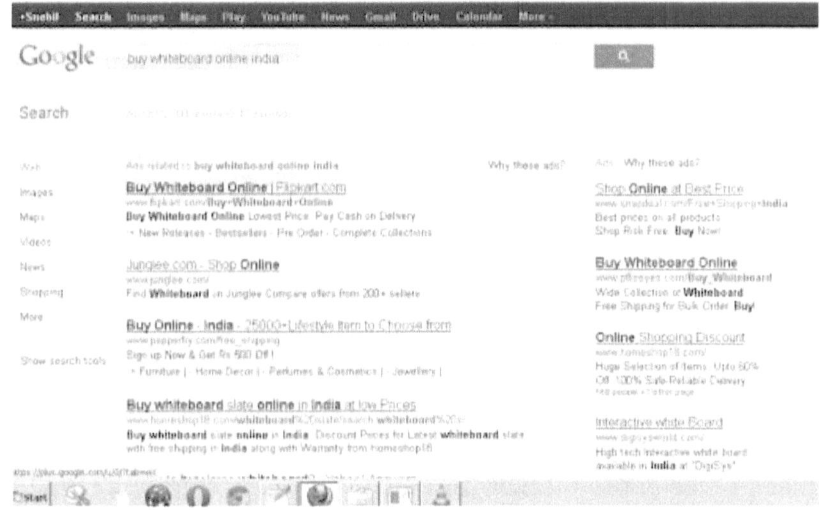

For E-Commerce platforms, Google Ads is a medium to drive the attention towards their platform by appearing on the search results of other platforms. With Amazon giving a neck to neck competition, getting your google ad copy is crucial. Flipkart uses 3rd party platforms to run ads and advertise on different websites, majorly to remarket to those customers who add products to their carts or just wishlist. Once a user clicks on any of their google ads, Flipkart re-targets them across social media platforms using the Facebook Pixel via ads.

Flipkart's Affiliate Program

Affiliate marketing is performance-based marketing by which a person can earn rewards in the form of commission for marketing another person's or company's products. Flipkart delegates the responsibility of marketing its products to third parties known as affiliates and shares a part of the profit on the sale of the products. Affiliate programs of e-commerce portals like Flipkart and Amazon are some of the legit ways to earn money online during this lockdown. Flipkart portal offers almost everything needed by a commoner. From beauty to baby care products to fashion to electronics and beauty to baby care products, everything can be found on this online portal. All you need is decent traffic on your website or blog. You can then join Flipkart's affiliate program and market a range of products of your niche. Flipkart offers one of the best affiliate marketing programs through which people are earning around Rs. 25,000 to Rs. 80,000 per month. -15% of the product's price.

Flipkart Affiliate Marketing Commission

Below we are mentioning a few product categories and their commission percentages:

Books and e-learning (10%)

Gold and silver coins (0.1%)

School supplies and toys (10%)

Baby care products (10%)

Fragrances and Beauty products (10%)

Household supplies (10%)

To know more about the commission percentage for each product category click here Affiliate programs are perfect for larger stores and e-Commerce sites, and this is one of the highly successful marketing strategies of Flipkart.

Youtube Marketing

With YouTube being reached as the world's second-largest search engine (behind Google) Flipkart completely leveraged this platform to advertise its marketing campaigns. Flipkart launched a targeted marketing campaign for the fashion segment known as "India ka Fashion Capital", focused on featuring video ads on youtube as most of their audience are present here. Google was also able to measure the impact of digital vs traditional media strategies, which made it clear that the brand had made a good bet by going all out on digital platforms.

Flipkart – Covid Strategy

The COVID-19 crisis has put everyone in a fix. During this time the demand for online services was high due to obvious reasons, so that Flipkart along with other e-commerce platforms had to deliver products keeping their safety as well as their customers' safety in mind.

To ensure the safety of their customers Flipkart started a no Contact Delivery process #FlipkartForIndia, where products will get delivered after proper sanitization and health & hygiene checking.

To appreciate and support the frontline warriors, Flipkart in collaboration with its parent company Walmart, donated medical supplies worth Rs 46 Cr to fight the battle against CoronaVirus in India. That's not all to get the essentials delivered to its customers safely and as soon as possible, Flipkart partnered with Uber and Meru Cabs in various cities across the country. Along with all this Flipkart #SmartBuy also launched hand sanitizers and surgical masks to ensure there's no shortage in this battle.

Flipkart didn't do all these just for their Brand Promotion and that's clear by the way they have promoted common people who were out on road as a support for the needy and the warrior on their Social Media Platform and labelled it as #FlipkartBrightSide. Flipkart shared stories of common people doing their bit, for example:

1. To aid the strenuous efforts taken by policemen in Kerala to enforce the lockdown, Anand and Sivan Macro offered them a tea break!The father-son duo set up a makeshift tea kiosk in their car, distributing nearly 200 cups of tea every day.

2. Renowned ophthalmologist Shibal Bhartiya in Delhi assembled a team of volunteers and has distributed over 2,000 packets of biscuits, 4,600kg of dal-chawal (uncooked), 2,000 soap cakes and 500kg detergent to the needy.

CASE 21

About Sugar Cosmetics-

Launched in 2015, Sugar Cosmetics is the fastest-growing premium cosmetics brand. This Indian brand was started by Vineeta Singh and her husband Kaushik Mukherjee. It was merely launched with two products i.e. A dark matte eyeliner and a dark kohl pencil. Today, this beloved brand deals in foundations, concealers, lipsticks, Eyeliner, Bronzers, Eyeshadow, Highlighters, etc enhancing the lips, eyes, face, nails, and skin tone of Indian women and men. The fact that they didn't restrict the brand to women merely, contributed enormously to its success. Being an Indian brand, they are keen on providing products meeting the exact requirement of Indian customers. From 2,500+ retail outlets in 2020 to 35,000+ across 130+ cities as of today, Sugar Cosmetics has come a long way! Sugar Cosmetics is keen on strengthening its Omni channel approach. This brand is targeted toward bold and independent women who do not restrict themselves to the typical and so-called stereotypes created by society.

How has Sugar corrected the cosmetics industry in India?

So, what makes Sugar Cosmetics different from others? Well, back in 2015, you could find Maybelline or Lakme products within the 300 rs range. Or, if you have a high budget and you are planning to buy products worth 1000 or more, then you have MAC Cosmetics and Estee! But the gap between 300 and 1000 was not acknowledged earlier. No brand had launched products within this price range. In order to bridge the gap, Sugar Cosmetics took the responsibility to sell products in this range. Plus, we mostly had international products based on Global

Skin standards. On getting in touch with several women, she found out that these international products don't suit our skin tone because Indian Skin type is different! No one took care of Indian pollution and skin type in mind before launching the products. Keeping all these things in mind, Sugar Cosmetics launched their Matte Range products that suited best their Indian customers.

The business model of Sugar Cosmetics-

- Sugar Cosmetics follows the D2C model for its business. Plus, it is keen on strengthening omnichannel performance.

- The company has an excellent distribution network operating in more than 130 cities with a retail presence of 35,000+ stores in India.

- Their model was mainly focused on Indian consumers who got problems with international brands. Hence, they made products that suited best to their Indian clients.

- If we talk about their revenue, in the past 3 years, the company's income has increased 7 times. For FY21, they earned a net income of 130 crores.

- Their major source of revenue are-direct sales in India and export sales across the world. Side by side, they earn from advertisements.

Marketing Strategy of Sugar Cosmetics-

Mid-Range products:

As we discussed earlier, Sugar Cosmetics was the first one to acknowledge the gap in the price range. If you go for Lakme or Maybelline products, the price range would be within 300. But, if you wish to buy products priced at 1000 or more, you have MAC and Estee for the same. But, the gap between 300 and 1000 remained intact, there were no products ranging between this. Sugar Cosmetic decided to bridge this gap and launched their products between 300 and 1000. These products were affordable and quickly caught the attention of customers.

Inclusivity:

Inclusivity played a major role in the promotion of Sugar Cosmetics. Anyone from professional background needs a 'touch-up'. The majority of men still call it 'touch-up' and not makeup since makeup on men is something that hasn't been normalized yet. Sugar has never restricted its brand to women only. Even men on various fronts need it, so their doors are open for all genders. Since their products are never gender specified, they didn't feel the need to introduce a separate brand.

Influencers marketing:

Well, everyone does Influencer marketing! What's different in this? So, Sugar cosmetics didn't merely rope in the influencers for marketing, but they turned the customers into influencers. If you are happy with the product, you won't mind flaunting it! So, in this case, Sugar Cosmetics convinced their customers to share their reviews on the product and uploaded them on Social media. Plus, they have always enjoyed free promotions. i.e Word of mouth marketing in simple terms. Since a happy customer is a good resource, they helped the brand to grow its customer base to a huge extent.

Hybrid Model (Online+ offline presence):

Until 2017, Sugar Cosmetics was a digital-only brand. They used to sell products through websites and other leading eCommerce partners. By early 2018, they got into general Trade and large-format retailers in shopping malls and then slowly started launching exclusive stores. Today, they sell their products via various eCommerce marketplaces like Sugar Cosmetics, Amazon, Nykaa, Shein, etc. Talking about their retail presence, they have 35,000 retail outlets in 130+ cities. they are trying their best to strengthen their omnichannel approach in every possible way.

Digital Marketing:

In order to reach the audience, digital marketing is perhaps the best option. Sugar Cosmetics too tried to market their product through this pathway. Out of all the digital platforms, Instagram and Youtube have worked wonders for them! Why? because they have that 'short video' option that sums up the whole of specifications in a few seconds. Since the scenario today has completely changed, people don't invest time in reading blogs, so they shifted towards short, crispy, and informative videos.

Now, in terms of content, who knows better than Sugar? Now that the content should be engaging, their reels are enriched with infotainment. i.e. Information and Entertainment since they use humor while informing the audience. As we know how short videos are working well in their favor, they are looking forward to collab with apps like Josh, Moj, and Takatak.

Leverage Social Media and Influencer Marketing techniques

Sugar, which has close to 1.5Mn followers on Instagram actively collaborates with influencers and engages with their audiences on different platforms apart from Instagram too. During an interview, upon asking how sugar leverages influencer marketing ROI and social media, Vineeta told that they believe in authenticity and work with influencers who genuinely love Sugar instead of popular influencers who will talk about Sugar today and someone else tomorrow. She said that Sugar experiments on different social media platforms like Moj and Chingaari, apart from Instagram, YouTube and Twitter. Sugar is quite popular on YouTube with huge subscribers.

Sugar works with influencers who genuinely love Sugar and don't talk about it only because they have to talk. They talk about it because they love it. And when they talk with authenticity, they exude the vibes which people can vibe on and they know that they are not being a fake influence.

Sugar takes things to the next level by transforming their customers into influencers.

When you're absolutely in love with a product, you can't help but show it off to the world! And that's exactly what Sugar Cosmetics has managed to achieve with their brilliant marketing strategy. By encouraging their customers to share their honest reviews on social media, the brand has been able to harness the power of word-of-mouth marketing, which is one of the most effective ways to grow a customer base.

And it's no surprise that their customers are happy to sing Sugar's praises - the brand's products are simply amazing! From their vibrant lipsticks to their stunning eyeshadows, Sugar Cosmetics has everything you need to look and feel your best. And when you combine that with their focus on customer satisfaction and engagement, it's no wonder that their customer base has grown to a massive extent.

Sugar has done its influencer marketing the right and innovative way, their stats tell that. It is growing with a CAGR of 25% even in these difficult times.

Truly, the secret to an ever-lasting influence on people is through authentic and genuine campaigns.

CASE 22

CASE STUDY: DIGITAL MARKETING FOR EDUCATION INDUSTRY

How Aarna Systems helped Sanskruti World School establish itself as a leading education brand in Boisar with Digital Marketing Strategies

Sanskruti World School, managed by Adhikari Group, brought world-class education to the suburbs of Mumbai – Boisar & Palghar. They offer CBSE Board education from Nursery to Grade X and have a Junior College on their campus for all three streams- Science, Commerce, and Arts. Their effective learning practices include creative thinking, communication, interactive learning and more. The school is committed to shaping students to be passionate learners, global citizens, and future-ready.

OBJECTIVES

Launching a comprehensive education hub in Boisar, our client's goal was to create brand awareness across Boisar and nearby suburbs, create a user-friendly school website, maximize brand engagement, increase admission inquiries, and establish the school as a credible education brand in the long run. We teamed up to achieve these goals and connect students better to education.

CHALLENGES

Imagine using Digital Marketing for a School located in the suburbs of Mumbai – Boisar & Palghar. For those unaware of this location, Boisar & Palghar has moderate literacy levels, and the locals majorly communicate in the regional Marathi language. People here are not very internet -savvy. Hence, it was difficult to convey the right message to the right audience through the right digital channel. While the Mumbai suburbs are at their developing stage, Boisar & Palghar already have some very reputed schools. The challenge was also to enter in direct competition with the well-established schools. To the top of it, the school started its first batch in the year 2020 (during the corona-virus pandemic lockdown). It was a very challenging task for the school and digital team to gain parents' trust in the newly opened school with the new normal – Online Classes.

OUR DIGITAL APPROACH

All the odds being on our side, we were confident about this project. Our digital team did a thorough analysis of the online behavior of people residing in our target locations – Boisar, Palghar and nearby areas. This helped us in determining the specific set of keywords to reach SEO goals. We designed and developed a responsive website, published blogs on education, life skills, and students' holistic development. We understood our target audience's social media behavior are majorly limited to Facebook and some fractions to Instagram & Twitter. For Social Media Marketing, we engaged the target audience with creative posts highlighting the school's facilities, advantages, awareness on the CBSE board, interesting facts, quiz questions, parenting tips, online school activities, admission updates and more. Our Paid Advertising experts used a strategic lead generation funnel for ads. We leveled the social media ads in various stages – Awareness, Consideration, Conversion to target and acquire leads efficiently.

THE IMPACT

SEO

After 6 months of implementing SEO strategies, Sanskruti World School's 7 out of 9 keywords ranked on the first page. Keyword 'English Primary School in Boisar' ranked in 2nd position. Keyword 'Nursery and Primary School' in Boisar ranked in 3rd position. The school's website started receiving good organic traffic, generating more admission inquiries and credibility. Indeed, our smart SEO efforts proved fruitful for the client.

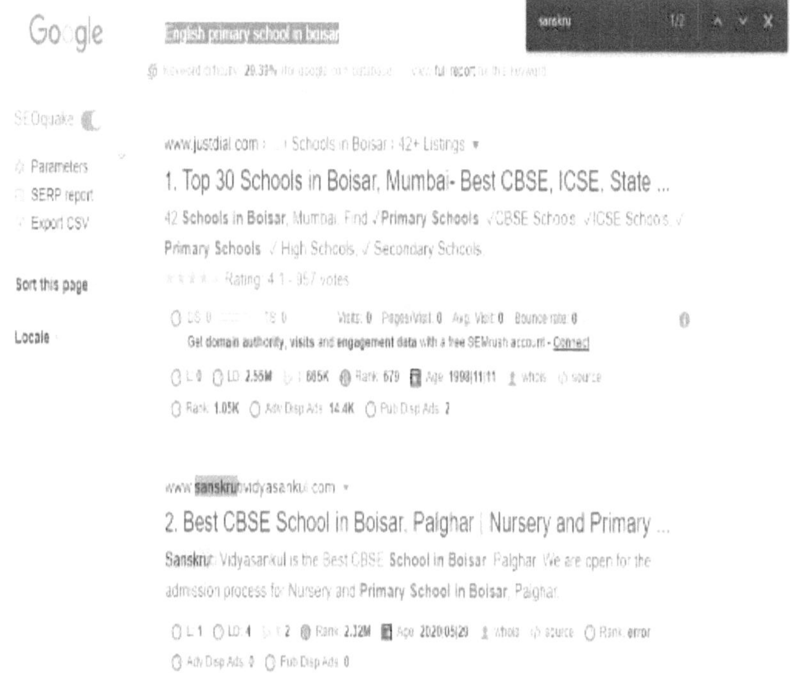

PAID ADS

Aarna Systems' smart digital advertising strategy poured in lots of admission enquiry leads for Sanskruti World School within a short span. It brought 589 Whatsapp Leads, 316 Website Call Leads, 192 leads filled the online form, etc. The avg. conversion rate exceeded the expectations. Ad campaigns with 688,299 Total Reach and 80,770 Post Engagement initiated school admissions successfully in 2020.

OUR AD CREATIVES

We ran the ads in two languages – English & Marathi for better targeting and conversion. Ad creatives were designed, keeping the target students' age group in mind.

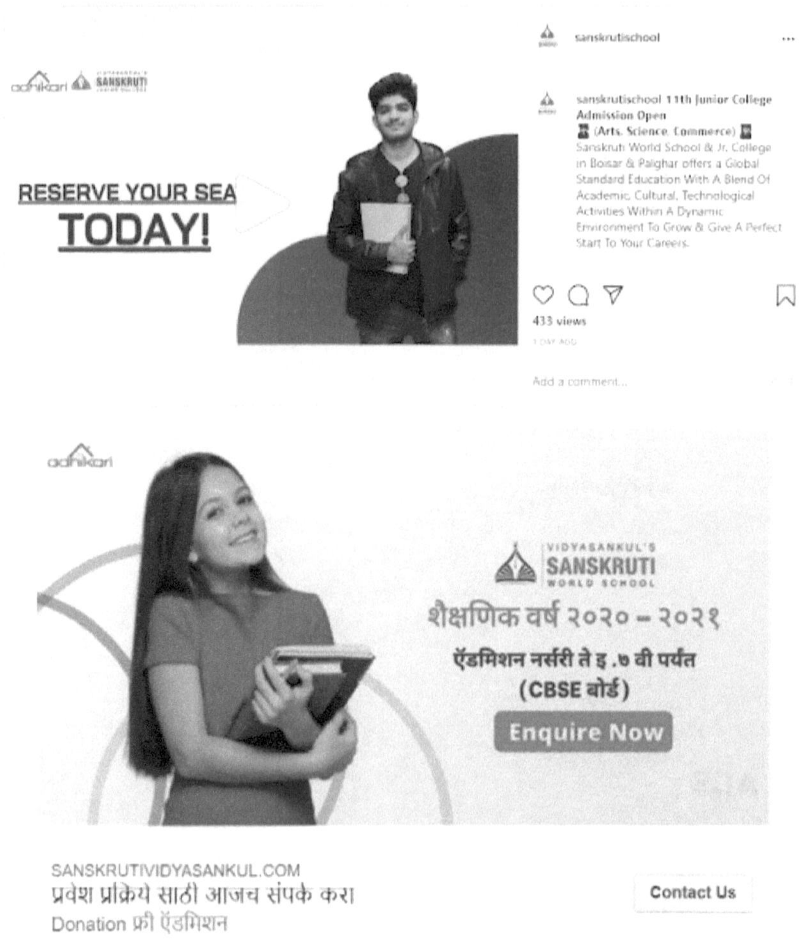

SOCIAL MEDIA

Our team brainstormed ways to keep the School active on Social Media – Facebook, Instagram & Twitter. Now, Sanskruti World School's official page is filled with interesting posts, quizzes, information, and learning motivation for students. Most of the traditional school setups in Boisar don't use social media marketing strategies actively. This earned a brownie point for Sanskruti World School. Now, the school is gaining attention & appreciation for its social media engagement.

SOCIAL MEDIA CREATIVES

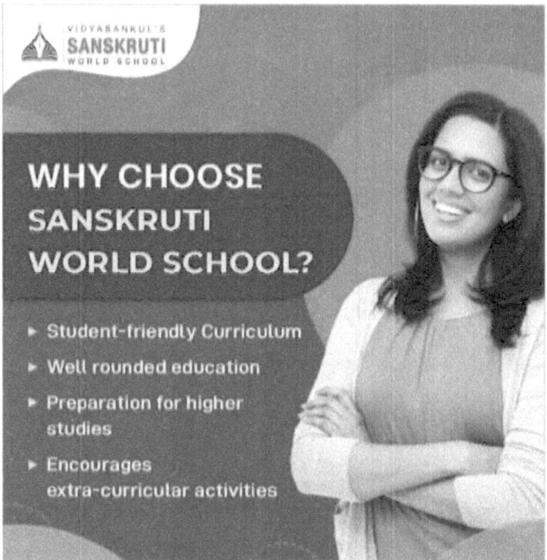

THE RESULT

Today, Sanskruti World School is a well-known educational institution in the Mumbai Suburbs-Boisar & Palghar. The year 2020 was challenging for all. However, it did not stop our client from stepping into the education sector with sheer determination, exclusive technology and smart digital marketing services. People of Boisar got engaged through our subtle digital marketing strategy at the initial stage. Despite being pandemic, the school admissions kept rising till September 2020 and finally school had to close the admission. Imagine the overwhelming response for a newly opened. The school conducted online classes, celebrated online events and this also helped in gaining parents' trust. In just one year, the school managed to establish a brand voice and recognition in Boisar and nearby areas. Our digital activities helped the client to gain the edge over the competitors. Our experts gave the school a brand identity and it sets it apart from the well-established schools in Boisar. Now the next batch of admission have started and the school portals are again filled with admission inquiries. We are glad!

Balancing our strategy with the target location and audience took a careful observation and analysis, carried out by our seasoned digital experts. being a leading digital marketing company in Pune, Aarna Systems believes it is just the beginning. As a team of digital experts, we are all set to help our client achieve incredible feats in the education sector.

CASE 23

The Loom

The stylish apparel frontrunner, The Loom, has been slaying the influencer marketing game with their drool-worthy Instagram feed. Many trendsetters showcase the brand's clothing and accessories range with pure finesse – be it a Bollywood celeb like Aishwarya Rai, Karisma Kapoor, or your everyday style icon, you'll find them shining bright in The Loom apparel!

Despite the mass appeal of celebrity endorsements, the company is still striving to make its collection more accessible through lesser-known influencers who are better able to connect with and inspire their target audience. In fact, the brand is embracing the power of influencers and showcasing them wearing their apparel on their website! Not only does it provide an opportunity for potential customers. to get inspired by creative, stylish looks, but it also boosts their own brand visibility – a double win!

CASE 24

Mama Earth

Mamaearth is blowing the lid off influencer marketing for eCommerce. With over 100 influencers tapped across various social media channels, Mamaearth's all-inclusive plan reaches both micro and macro-influencers alike. Some of Mamaearth's influencer campaigns like the "#ShaadiWalaGlowEveryday" with the stunning Shilpa Shetty Kundra were incredible successes. And in 2021, the brand has been proudly represented by Sara Ali Khan, giving Mamaearth a chic modern edge.

Additionally, partnering with mom bloggers and influencers has granted the brand an aura of desirability, and as a result, the overall value of our brand has skyrocketed. Checkout their "Goodness is a Choice" campaign where Insta Mom's shared their experience of using Mamaearth's beauty products.

CASE 25

LENSKART

In the age of online shopping, Lenskart is leading the way with their digital presence. With over 1.5 million followers on Facebook and 677K followers on Instagram, they have leveraged their strong social media presence to drive sales and attract shoppers.

Not only does the company invest in traditional forms of advertising such as TV and print ads, but they also invest in influencer marketing to make sure that more customers get to know about them.

In one of its influencer campaigns, Lenskart sent a fashionable pair of shades to actor Katrina Kaif who subsequently posted a dazzling photo of herself wearing them on her Instagram account. Her post captured the attention of viewers everywhere, causing an immense surge in the number of visitors to Lenskart's website.

Another influencer campaign that strike the right chords with the audience was the #Halkarakhyaar campaign launched in October 2019 with influencer Bhuvan Bam as Lenskart's brand ambassador. To capture the modern and eclectic vibes of their new collection, Lenskart embraced a carefree way of life. Showcasing an unabashed sense of fashion, the campaign celebrates freedom and style!

CASE 26

film

Social Media to Promote Movies

PAD MAN

If you're a frequent 'grammar, you must have seen your favourite celebs holding a sanitary napkin, along with the hashtag, #PadManChallenge. The campaign which was started by its lead actors, Akshay Kumar and Sonam Kapoor and producer, Twinkle Khanna became a HUGE rage on Instagram. Not only Bollywood actors, but also well-known sports person and singers, and even fans took up the challenge on social media. The challenge was so successful that it taught people about menstrual hygiene and that 'there's no shame in holding a pad, it's natural, it's just blood. Period.' (sic) Kudos to Twinkle Khanna for bringing such an important subject on screen and Arunachalam Muruganantham who's life story was the inspiration behind the movie and the entire movement.

PHILLAURI

Anushka Sharma's second venture as a producer, Phillauri saw her playing the role of a friendly ghost. To drive excitement for her movie, Anushka started a rather funny digital marketing strategy before the release of the movie—it is also touted to have one of the most innovative movie marketing campaigns in recent times. The marketing strategy revolved around around the plot of the movie, which saw Shashi (Anushka's character in the movie) present at some of the most iconic moments in the past.

Samsung is one of the international firms that are successful in identifying changes, reacting to them, and giving appropriate solutions in today's quickly expanding globe. It was founded in 1938 and is now one of the world's most valuable brands, delivering a wide range of electrical devices. Samsung is the largest chaebol in South Korea, with multiple related businesses, the majority of which are grouped under the Samsung brand. It has the eighth-greatest worldwide brand value as of 2020.

CASE 27

DIGITAL PRESENCE OF SAMSUNG

Samsung's success in digital marketing can be attributed to its adept use of social currency to achieve corporate results. Customers' level of engagement with a brand, as well as their readiness to share knowledge with others, is characterized as social currency. By extending its social media presence, Samsung has done its best to provide customers and brand loyalists with the chance to share their Samsung experience with those in their circle—friends and family members. Brands like Samsung must speak to the interests and concerns of the many segments of the population that their products target. This means they have social profiles on all of the major social networks. Samsung has done a commendable job on the same and is well-represented on all major social media sites, including Facebook, Twitter, YouTube, and Instagram. Through its specialized social media pages, Samsung has very attentive and committed customer care teams available.

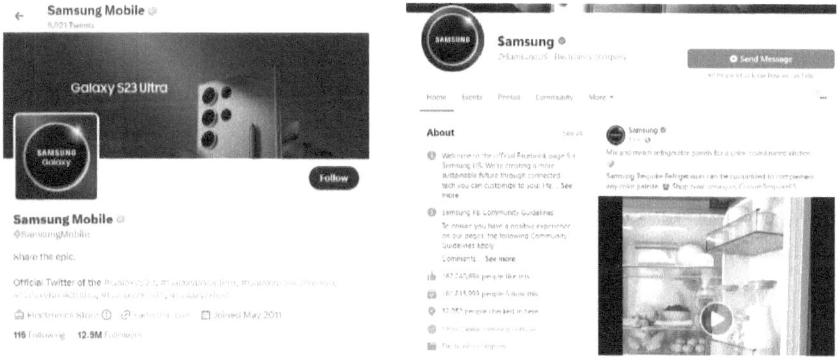

CASE 28

Digital Marketing Campaigns of Samsung

Samsung has positioned itself to be a community-oriented brand impacting audiences worldwide by introducing various marketing campaigns. Along with a promising marketing strategy Samsung also does a great job in promoting its products and appealing its audience with exceptional marketing campaigns. Recently during Pride Month, the brand celebrated with the community displaying with pride the importance of diversity and how Samsung stands as an ally for the LGBTQ++ community on its Social Media handles. This content strategy is known as UGC or User-Generated Content. Enjoy having a look at these exceptional Marketing Campaigns by Samsung.

CASE 29

CCD

With the help of social media and use of YouTube, CCD managed to reach a huge proportion of their target audience, increased brand awareness and engagement, and increased intent to buy. What's more, a huge proportion of this success can be attributed directly to the use of social media and, above all else, YouTube.

Strategy Adopted

Café coffee day, made coffee drinking popular among Indian youth by offering a brand experience environment and other value addition. They started by providing Internet facilities initially at the cafe', during the year 2000, when internet was not easily accessible. They targeted the youth around the ages between 16-29 years and created a hangout place for a chit chat kind of experience. Since social media is most popular among the youth, they decided to advertise only Digitally. That is only with the help of digital marketing, they wanted to gain as many customers as possible.

Platform-wise strategy: -

Facebook: Content-wise they are focused on promoting Cafe' Coffee Day as a place to have conversations. Aptly supported by some good photography, they have expressive image updates to resonate with the vibrancies on youngsters with good copy editing abilities of the team which writes their updates as well.

The Sit Down campaign is doing a good job at creating a buzz around the Internet. Thanks to their catchy YouTube video and the nice music, people have taken up to the concept of 'Sit Down'. About their cafe', new menu, offers and events are conveyed through Social media. They are also focused on providing the best service at the cafe' so that there isn't, even a single negative remark by customers.

In Facebook, with 2 updates every day, they seem to be getting quite a good traction from their community. For a brand with more than 3 million people in its community, they boast a healthy 9% fan engagement for a month. We all know how difficult it is to get such traction when you have a really huge user base. Having generated more than 260k fan interactions in the 30 days, they are one of the most engaging Indian brands on Facebook. While, a huge chunk of these fan interactions are 'likes' but they are also able to pull off a lot many comments as well, which is a difficult ask.